MODELLING
SAILING
MEN-OF-WAR

MODELLING SAILING MEN-OF-WAR

An Illustrated Step-by-Step Guide

Philip Reed

Naval Institute Press

This Book is dedicated to

PAT

without whose patience, hard work and sense of humour this book
would never have been completed,

and to

NORMAN OUGH AND DONALD McNARRY

For much of the inspiration
that has sustained and guided me through the years

First published in Great Britain in 2000 by
Chatham Publishing,
61 Frith Street,
London W1V 5TA

Chatham Publishing is an imprint of Gerald Duckworth & Co Ltd

Published and distributed in the United States of America and Canada by
the Naval Institute Press, 291 Wood Road, Annapolis, Maryland 21402-5034

Library of Congress Catalog No. 00-104256

ISBN 1-55750-444-X

This edition is authorized for sale only in the United States,
its territories and possessions, and Canada.

Manufactured in Great Britain.

CONTENTS

Acknowledgements	6
The Ship	7
Introduction	9
The Workshop	12
Building the Model	
The Hull	15
Channels and Chainplates	32
Decks and Armament	39
The Belfry	65
The Stern	66
The Bow and Figurehead	75
Carronades, Ropes and Boats	81
Hammock Netting and Other Details	92
Carving the Sea	96
Masts, Spars, Yards and Rigging	99
The Rigging Plan	112
Anchors and Stern Lanterns	118
Flags	120
Photographing the Model	120
Materials and Tools	122
Bibliography	124

ACKNOWLEDGEMENTS

Writing this book has been a labour of love, which would have been made much more difficult without the help and support from many people. For this reason the author wishes to express his gratitude to the following organisations and individuals.

To the National Maritime Museum research department who did the research on the *Majestic* for me; also to the staff of the museum who, in the past, have helped me to photograph the models in their care.

To all those at Geoff Marshall Photographics of 4 Cathedral Lane, Truro, who have been so helpful in processing all the photographs used in the book.

To Rod and Carol Langton for their continued friendship as well as their encouragement and support whilst writing this book (and the use of their very extensive reference library!). To Michael Wall of the American Marine Gallery, Salem, who over the years has been both friend and agent for my work. To my good friend Norman Swales for his help researching the model and obtaining some of the materials that I have used to carry out the project. To John Bowen editor of *Model Shipwright* for his ever present help and support.

To Norman Ough and Donald McNarry – all of us working in this field today owe them a great debt.

Last, but not least, Pat Cole who tirelessly and patiently has taken my scribblings, translated them into English and put them onto the word processor; she deserves a medal.

THE SHIP

HMS *Majestic* – A 74-gun ship

HMS *Majestic* was built from a William Batley draught first drawn up in 1759 for HMS *Canada* but revived after Batley's retirement in 1765. She was built by Adams and Barnard and launched at Deptford in 1785. *Majestic* was a common class 74-gun ship and at 1,642 tons her keel was 141ft long and the beam 46ft 9in and she carried a crew of six hundred men. Her armament consisted of thirty 32pdrs, thirty 18pdrs and fourteen 9pdrs. In addition, she may have carried some carronades at certain stages of her career. The plans show the poop rail adapted to receive at least four.

Majestic was commissioned in 1790 and, under Captain Cotton, she was present at the Glorious 1st of June in 1794. She saw action under various captains from 1795 to 1809 and together with *Daedalus* and *Incendiary* sank *Le Suffren* off Brest in 1796 and alone captured *El Bolador* in 1797. On 1st August 1798 she took part in the battle of the Nile.

In 1812 *Majestic* was reduced to a frigate with twenty-eight 32pdrs, twenty-eight 42pdr carronades and one 12pdr chase gun. She then saw further action capturing *La Terpischore* and *Dominica* in 1814 and taking part in the capture of the US *President* in 1815 before being decommissioned and finally broken up in 1816.

INTRODUCTION

My earliest experience of ship models, indeed the only one that I can now remember from childhood, was when I was taken to the National Maritime Museum at Greenwich, and found myself mesmerised by the models with their exposed timbers, separate planks and brass cannons; I longed to be able to make something like that myself, but it was to be many years before I began modelling. After studying, and then teaching, Fine Art in the 1960s I came to ship modelling almost by accident.

In 1971 I bought a plastic kit of USS *Constitution* as a Christmas present for a friend, more as a joke than anything else, and ended up building it myself – not very well if I remember. I then came across *Plank on Frame Models* by Harold Underhill in a local library and started work on a ¼in to 1ft (¹⁄₄₈ scale) brig to some of his plans. These two events amounted to something of a Damascene revelation for me. I became so passionate about my models and so absorbed in them that for years I went nowhere without a miniature tool kit and the fittings from the current project to work on when ever time and space were available. I also haunted bookshops and museums, slowly accumulating reference material and knowledge and becoming drawn ever deeper into the subject.

The museums I loved. They were full of models in cases that you could walk around, enabling detailed examinations to be made and photographs to be taken. Access was free and copies of original draughts cost only a few shillings. Books on the subject were, however, in very short supply and it seems incredible, when one peruses the book lists of today, that thirty years ago so few specialist publications were available.

In 1972 I moved to Cornwall, to another teaching post, and continued to build models during my spare time. Looking back I think this 'spare time' amounted to considerably more hours per week than were spent earning a living. In 1977 I started on a series of ¹⁄₃₂ in to 1ft (¹⁄₃₈₄ scale) World War II warships and early the following year made my first sale: a model of the battlecruiser HMS *Hood*. Various commissions followed and at the end of 1982 I left teaching to try to make a living from modelmaking. This was a decision I have never regretted, but anyone contemplating such a move should heed the warning given by Donald McNarry in his introduction to *Ship Models in Miniature*. 'When an amateur I remember writing to the late Mr Norman Ough and delicately skirting round the subject, and with professional common sense he said that the work had to look worth £1 per hour and if it got a quarter of this one was lucky. This was twenty years ago and the principle is the same today.' It is just as pertinent a further twenty-five years on.

From those early days I have never lost my love of, and total commitment to, ship models. I had worked hard and experimented endlessly during my college years but had never really felt at home with any of the media I was working with until I discovered model building. I do not really view it just as a craft, a career or a way of earning a living, but as a way of life and an art form which uses my particular talents and in which I can totally immerse myself.

At one end of the spectrum, of course, a ship model may well be no more than an exercise in craftsmanship or, indeed, just an object produced for sale. There are models, however, that are palpable works of art, expressions of their creators' visions. We need look no further than the models of Norman Ough and Donald McNarry to understand that a ship model can sometimes not only be admired as a work of skilful craftsmanship but can also have the power to move, inspire and involve. Ships are fascinating, complex and beautiful forms and the aim should be not only to reproduce that beauty faithfully but also add that intangible something extra that breathes life into the work. This involves questioning everything, rejecting and frequently reworking; it involves taking texture, tone and colour into account, and being aware of wind, wave, light and weather and much else besides. A model must be accurate but it must also 'feel right'.

I approach my modelling much as I did my painting thirty years ago, though it is, of course, far more structured and restrictive. For one thing, the plans and tables have to be adhered too. One needs technical expertise with many different materials, and over and above this there is the continual 'willing into being' of a picture already formed in the imagination. But I want to stress also the need for discipline and application without which a love affair with a fascinating subject could end up as a one-night stand. I remember so clearly my passionate involvement with the first models I built and, despite inevitable ups and downs, this passion has remained with me. All that I can I give to my work and I have had much in return. Every model I build is different and there are stages in the building of all of them where I struggle, but there are also long periods when the hours effortlessly melt away. Time and the world outside become increasingly distant, and I enter an almost contemplative state where extraneous thoughts rarely disrupt the flow of work; it is here that the real rewards lie.

*   *   *

I had it in mind for many years to put together a book detailing some of the techniques I have used to build my miniature models. I have written a few articles outlining many of these techniques but I have often been asked if I could go into greater depth and for this, I believed, a book was needed. On surveying the published books, however, it seemed that there was already a plethora of manuals and useful 'how-to' titles and I felt that it would be pointless to write something which merely reproduced what had already been done so well, with only my own preferences and prejudices added. Over a period I came to feel that what would be of interest and help to others would be, not a written description of a selection of techniques but rather a pictorial diary of the day-to-day construction of one model from start to finish. I also felt that photographs would explain more clearly than text alone many of the processes involved, and that by adhering to the discipline of photographing every stage of the work I would avoid the gaps so frustratingly found in some manuals.

To produce these photographs I had to work a lot of the time with a single lens reflex camera on a tripod. It was frequently squeezed between myself and the work and operated by a foot-operated control. This homemade contraption became so restrictive and irritating, that after a while I resorted to timed exposures for those occasions when one or both hands had to be in the picture. In addition, room was needed for at least one floodlight on a stand. The earlier photographs were taken using whatever light was available, but the depth of field was restricted so that I subsequently set up lighting for each shot.

At the time of making a start on *Majestic* I had, for some time, been planning to build a typical 74-gun ship of the Napoleonic era, to a slightly larger scale than I had previously used, incorporating one or two very different techniques to those usually employed when building a true miniature. It is neither what can usually be considered a full size model nor is it a true miniature. The project was to be, to some extent, ground breaking for me and would involve techniques and methods that I had not used before. I have always found it beneficial to switch between scales; it not only

keeps interest in the subject fresh but develops new skills and sharpens your problem-solving abilities. An instance of this was when, early on in my career, I switched from working at ½in to 1ft (⅟₈₄ scale) to ⅟₁₆in to 1ft (⅟₇₂ scale). At the larger scale it was obvious that a greater amount of detail could be included and, being used to very fine work, this meant adding everything short of the nuts and bolts. When I returned to working at the smaller scale I found that I was loath to omit details that could easily be included at the larger scale. This is but one way in which we can learn and develop. Certainly, when it comes to rigging I have learnt much from rigging sailing ships that has been useful on modern warships and surprisingly, vice versa.

For the modelmaker a 74-gun ship is a complex subject. There is the subtle hull shape with its variety of planking. There are cannons and carronades in abundance, and a selection of boats – a launch, two different pinnaces as well as 25ft and 18ft cutters. There are the complex head works culminating in a figurehead and a decorative and intricate stern. Then there are the masts, spars and the seemingly endless details associated with a fully rigged ship of this period. This book, however, is not simply intended as a manual from which to build HMS *Majestic*, though it could be used as such certainly. While a 74 is quite a considerable undertaking the techniques demonstrated are suitable for many smaller craft, working at this or, indeed, smaller or larger scales.

Majestic is the third model of a 74 I have built. The first was a ½in to 1ft model of *Hercules* built sixteen years ago, followed by a ⅟₁₆in to 1ft model of *Warrior* two years later. At the time of building I had obviously undertaken a fair amount of research, and so I already had a working knowledge for approaching a model of a 74. I do recall, however, the apprehension I felt at the prospect of overcoming some of the more demanding problems unique to these ships. The secret of success lies in, first, obtaining good plans and other research material and, second, in thoroughly familiarising yourself with the ships by photographing and making drawings of other models. The best of these have to be the Navy Board models of the period. All those years ago when I was researching, the collections at the National Maritime Museum at Greenwich and the Science Museum at South Kensington were superbly displayed and accessible to the researcher and modelmaker. Most of them could be viewed from all angles as they were in individual cases and usually well lit, often by natural light. If some aspect of a model could not easily be seen there was usually a friendly curator who was prepared to open the case and reposition the model. Such access to models is no longer so easy to find. All too often a model is now presented in gloomy half light with one or two mini spot lights picking out 'features of interest'. This might be pretty for the casual visitor with a penchant for window shopping but it is not so useful for the serious researcher. Photography is not as easily carried out as it used to be and advanced written permission has usually to be obtained from any museum you intend to visit.

Various commissions and projects had kept me away from such an ambitious undertaking as a 74 for many years, though I had made some plans in my head and also collected various draughts for another model. The catalyst which got me started was the restoration I was doing of a prisoner-of-war model. I particularly enjoyed some of the work on the rigging, using fine thread and a home-made rope walk. It was all so much closer to real-life practice than my usual method of using wire alone for the rigging. Whilst doing the work I had ideas of combining, where appropriate, the two methods – rope and wire – on a model built to a slightly larger scale than my usual true miniature. At this slightly larger scale some full size practice could be used for some of the work but for many tasks I would still employ the basic techniques of the miniaturist. The scale I finally settled on was ³⁄₃₂in to 1ft (¹⁄₁₄₄) and this gave me a hull 19in long and a model with an overall length of 28in.

I used original draughts of the *Majestic* obtained from the National Maritime Museum. These are not only used for constant reference, but copies are made and mounted on card for preparing templates. The hull was formed from two blocks of wood and I chose jelutong which is stable and easy to carve. Its only vice is its rather open grain but as the hull was to be planked this was not going to pose a problem. I usually carve my hulls open down to the lower gundeck, subsequently fitting and detailing each deck from above. For this model, however, I adapted the excellent method propounded by Donald McNarry for his hull of the *Royal Oak* in which he employed two separate blocks of wood, hollowing out from the centreline. Whereas McNarry hollowed out the whole interior and later fitted individual planked decks mounted on card, I, working at the slightly larger scale, removed the wood from between each of the decks leaving these as part of the hull. I also made sections of the upper decks removable in order to gain access to those areas below when adding detail.

After some consideration as to which point in *Majestic*'s career I would depict, I decided to show her as she might have appeared at about the time of the battle of the Nile in 1798. My two previous models of 74-gun ships were both depicted at a somewhat earlier date with black whales and ochre sides. With *Majestic* I decided to show her with two ochre bands following the lines of the gunports. According to information found in Dr Frank Howard's book *Sailing Ships of War 1400-1860*, at the time of the battle of the Nile it was noted by Colonel Fawkes, who was present, that she was painted in this way. It is not made clear, however, whether this meant the black strake followed the line of the middle wale or whether, in fact, the yellow bands followed the line of the gunports and this is still open to conjecture. I tend to the belief that at this period it is likely that many of these ships would have had bands following the line of the gunports. Certainly, artists working in the late eighteenth and nineteenth centuries support this view and, in addition, there is a very fine modern watercolour of Nelson's Santa Cruz squadron at sea in 1797, by Derek Gardner, that favours this configuration. I decided to keep the topsides a plain black with no decorative work picked out, and I think that during wartime this would probably have been the case.

I was unable to amass much material about *Majestic*'s appearance at this time. It is unfortunate that the Admiralty Progress Books show no major alterations, only periodic repairs and/or replacement to her coppering and general maintenance. Exactly what this routine maintenance would have involved is not made clear, but it must be presumed that it included changes such as the raising of the walkways and sheerline at the waist of the ship.

As for the poop deck I do not know if the bulwarks were built up or not, but I chose to keep the original open rail. I believe this would be correct. I do have a copy of an original print of the period depicting *Majestic* at the battle of the Nile. It shows her stern from the port quarter, and most of her broadside is obscured by smoke and the stern by fallen top hamper. The ochre bands follow the gunports and she has an open rail to her poop. This appears to be covered with netting. However, this print, while useful cannot be relied upon as gospel.

I fitted four carronades on the poop. They add interest, the plans show her pierced to accommodate them, and they formed part of the armament of most 74s of the period. I prepared my own masting and rigging plan using dimensions from Lees' *Masting and Rigging*, photographs of the model of HMS *Hercules* in the National Maritime Museum and another plan I had previously prepared for HMS *Warrior*. Little needed changing other than alterations that would probably have been made to her rig by the late 1790s. The old, suitably altered plan for *Warrior* can be seen in some of the photographs. I continually made notes on this and brought it up to date as I proceeded through the rigging of the model. I then redrew a plan for inclusion in the book.

THE WORKSHOP

I certainly have a healthy curiosity, a fascination even, with the workshops of other modelmakers, and I'm sure we all share this trait to a greater or lesser extent..

My workshop was never really planned; it just grew with changing needs. The present layout was decided upon four years ago when refitting, but even then the main aim was to get back in business as soon as possible. Although the room is small, 13ft by 10ft, it is packed with tools, materials and half finished work. Most of the tools and materials which I use routinely I can lay my hands on without leaving my chair. The raised workbench with its adjustable arm rest plus the fully adjustable chair are all recent additions. I would certainly recommend anyone who spends long hours doing exacting work to think carefully about the ergonomics of a workshop.

Central to any workshop is the bench. Several years ago I raised my bench by 6½in by adding the box-like

structure shown. It measures 3in by 8in. A couple of battens secured to the bench stop it moving back and forth but it slides easily to the right to expose my woodworker's vice on the solid bench beneath. On the front of the bench I have fitted a padded arm rest which helps to take the strain off the upper arms, shoulders and neck. It is adjustable in both directions using some hefty wing nuts. It has proved very satisfactory not only for its designed function but also as a repository for tools, and a catchment area for all those little fittings that get dropped and end up on the floor. Combined with a fully adjustable chair, it provides a reasonable amount of flexibility in order to cope with the greatly differing, and sometimes very demanding, tasks which have to be carried out. At the back of the bench is a shelf with a bookrest for books, research notes or plans.

Placed centrally on the bench is a clear cutting mat, my preferred work surface. To the left of this (I am left handed) are the various tools being used at the time and behind these the paints, glues and varnishes. To the right of the bench there is the Minicraft transformer and beneath this a set of draws for tools.

For lighting, in addition to the fixed fluorescent tubes, I have the two adjustable lamps over the bench. One of these is fitted with a length of vacuum cleaner hose which is connected to my dust extraction unit. It is held in place with elastic bands but is adjustable and can be used over this area and also over the saw, lathe and sander on the reverse side of the bench. The vacuum drive itself is actually housed in a cupboard in the next room, so it is virtually silent.

On the reverse side of the bench is the Preac saw and behind it the lathe and sander. As can be seen, both light and dust extraction can easily be swung into place. The large and ungainly white tube rising beside and overhanging the bench is connected to an extractor fan located in the roof space. This is only a very recent addition and it is particularly useful for extracting unwanted fumes. If working with anything more than minute amounts of super glue, or some of the more unpleasant solvents, I position the inlet of the extractor over the palette dish or piece of glass that holds the offending substance and the fumes are removed. It is also useful when airbrushing. I have a home-made spray booth that sits on the bench during

use. It is made from a cut-down polystyrene fish box and in the back of it I have cut a hole that accepts the end of the extractor tube. When working on smaller items it deals quite adequately with the overspray. Immediately behind the chair is another workbench and display area. This one is usually covered with the current research material while higher still is a shelf holding models at various stages of completion.

The drawers underneath this bench hold drills, burrs, punches, rulers, prepared shavings, paints, lengths of prepared painted wire rigging, detail work for current models and much more. The drawers keep me organised and after years of accumulating so many bits and pieces I could not function comfortably without them.

At the far end of the workshop is more bench space and a shelf, on which is located the home-made rope walk and, beneath, on the right, my timber store. I have mounted on this bench a vice; this usually holds an old drill gauge that I use as a draw plate for producing dowels down to size 80. For finer dowels I use a series of tin draw plates that I made myself.

On the bench to the left is a box. It is open on the far side and has a removable top. It houses the grinder for sharpening and polishing tools. I use a 'green wax'

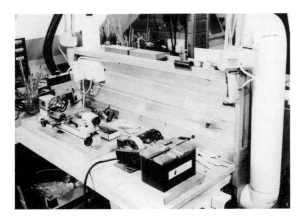

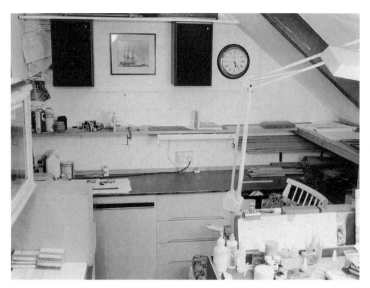

duck (one handed, with the blank in a vice) I found out about, and then obtained a selection of, burrs and cutters from a decoy duck carving catalogue. I have since used a selection of these for an amazing variety of jobs while building ship models and augment them with some much finer ones obtained from a dental tool supplier. One of the real 'finds', that has revolutionised my hollowing out of miniature models, has been the Carbide Cutters. These will remove wood quickly, easily, and accurately in the most inaccessible areas. The smaller and finer ones are ideal when used in the smaller Minicraft drills. They are not cheap, but they really do work.

I must emphasise that I now build models professionally and that the tools I have accumulated over the years take a lot of the strain out of the work as well as saving a great deal of time. However, when I first started it was a very different story and the tools I had available were very basic: a few hand tools, a pin vice for drilling and a domestic power drill in a vice for a lathe. This meant that in those early days, building plank-on-frame models, I had to find someone to cut my available timber into stock sheets and planks and from these all the timbers and fittings for my models had to be laboriously sawn, planed and otherwise shaped by hand. It was certainly a useful apprenticeship but may now be a thing of the past due to the availability of so many specialised power tools. Whether or not this is a good or bad thing only time will tell.

as a polishing agent and the box stops it getting everywhere.

To the left of my workbench is my library, extensive enough to enable me to solve most of the day-to-day research problems. Beneath these shelves is the 'office' area, the hi-fi (of sorts) and, of course, those two essential pieces of equipment, the kettle and the teapot.

I have a Unimat lathe, a good selection of Minicraft drills together with a very recent acquisition, the Preac circular saw. This is so accurate it has revolutionised some of my methods.

A few years ago, after breaking my arm in an accident and finding myself unable to build ship models, I discovered decoy duck carving and while carving my first

BUILDING THE MODEL

The Hull

1.

The two blocks of jelutong selected for the hull are being planed and squared. You can see that the raised workbench has been moved to one side to expose my vice. When it comes to timber – particularly when working to a larger scale – I prefer to use jelutong; it is easy to work and very stable and though it is a little fragile and easily damaged, repairs are easy. In this case it will be planked over and so it does not really represent a problem.

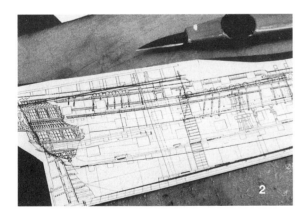

2.

For the templates I use copies taken from the plans. These have been mounted on card and this profile is now ready for cutting out. The outline I am going to cut to has been marked in. This includes a double line for the decks to define their camber; the upper line represents the height of the deck amidships and the lower the height at the ship's side. Both are marked to the top of the beams beneath the planking. The template is then cut out along the upper line.

3.

The profile template has been cut out and is being used to mark in the positions of the station lines.

4.

Using a sharp awl I am marking in the level of the gun-deck. This is then repeated on the other block of wood, turning the template over and using the same holes. The template is, of course, lined up on the blocks using the station lines.

5.
Using a simple doweling kit four dowels are fitted below the level of the gundeck. The two blocks can now be separated and re-assembled as often as wished with perfect alignment. It is a good idea to check that the dowels will not be in the way of the holes which will later to be drilled for the masts.

6.
The outline profile is now marked on the inside face of the blocks along with the station lines. I am using a template for these station lines as they are **not** at right angles to the base of the model (the waterline) but are at right angles to the keel which on this vessel is different. Always study the plans to check whether the waterline is parallel with the keel. It is frequently deeper aft.

7.
I have now carefully cut out all the gunports on the template and am marking their position on the outside of both blocks

8.
Using a drill press all the gunports are being centrally located.

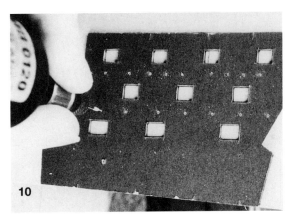

9.
The blocks are turned over and, on the inside surface, the top levels of all the decks are being marked in with a sharp point in a Minicraft drill, drilling through the template at regular intervals.

10.
Again, the template is reversed and the same process repeated with the other block, but this time drilling through the existing holes.

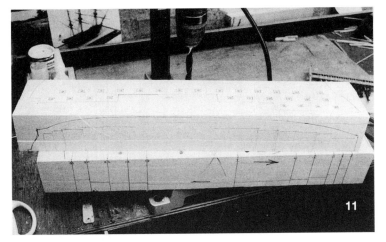

11.
On the upper surface of the block the maximum breadth of the ship has been marked in using a template. Within this outline there are some fainter horizontal lines between each of the station lines. These represent the maximum depth to which to drill when initially hollowing out between the decks. The drill press can then be set to drill to this depth and no further. The depth will vary from deck to deck because of the tumble-home. Regular checking and recalculating is therefore required.

12.
Starting to remove the wood.

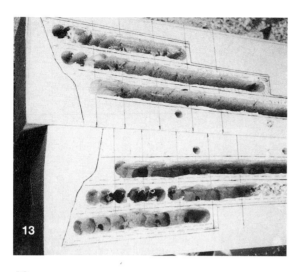

13.
The initial drilling out between the decks has been completed.

14.
It is a good idea at this stage to drill a couple of holes in the base which will later take the threaded rods that will eventually be used to secure the model in place in its carved sea.

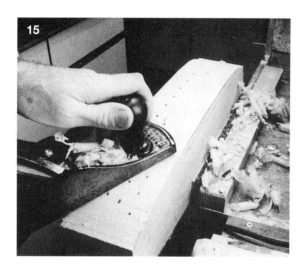

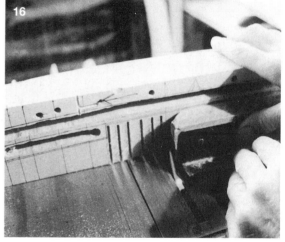

15.
The hull block has now been cut out in plan on the band saw and is being finished by plane.

16.
The profile of the ship being cut. This can be done in various ways though I prefer to make a series of cuts with the circular saw and then remove the wood with a chisel. The decks should only be cut down to the mid-ship level at this stage. Note in this photograph that now the hole drilled for the fixing rod has been extended with a right-angle ground out with a carbide bit. The screwed rod will be bent at a right-angle before being glued in place.

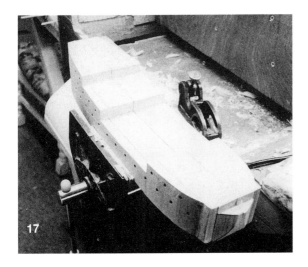

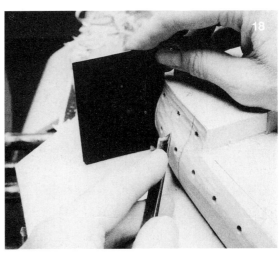

17.
Finishing the decks with a little bullnose plane.

18.
Card templates for each of the station lines have been prepared in the same way as those for the plan profile. I start amidships and work my way towards the bow and stern. For this job I use a ¾in chisel, a ½in gouge, a small violin maker's plane and the ever-useful bullnose plane.

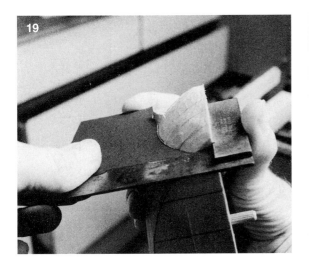

19.
I have cut the base of my templates level with the base line for the model so, with the model on a flat surface, they can be offered up to the broadside. If the model is held in a vice, as shown here, a square is employed to enable the template to be accurately located.

20.
During the whole process of carving a model I keep re-marking the station lines. This helps for positioning the templates, but, more importantly, provides a visual check on symmetry. I use templates and check dimensions regularly but in the end work by eye and feel. 'If it looks right it is right' is an old adage that should be borne in mind throughout the work.

21.
The rough shaping of the hull is finished.

22.
The hull seen from above.

23.
The profile template is trimmed down to the lower of the two deck lines and is used to re-delineate the deck level on the broadside. The camber is here being cut in using the bullnose plane.

24.
In order to ensure that the decks continue to line up perfectly I fit some little brass pins at intervals along the edges of the decks on one side of the hull only. The heads, with a small amount of super glue added, are inserted into pre-drilled holes, the pointed ends protruding no more than about a ⅟₁₆in. When the two halves of the model are reassembled, by pressing firmly together, they will make their own holes into which they will relocate each time the two halves are put back together. It is an very easy process and works very well.

25.
Here the bulwarks are being built up using more strips of jelutong. They are glued in place with little blobs of Seccotine so they can be easily broken off later on.

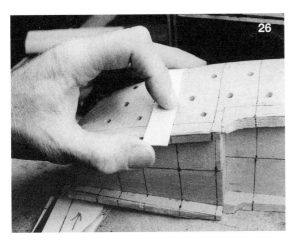

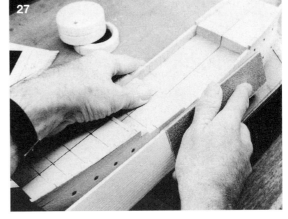

26.
Back to the carving and shaping. Here I am using a strip of plastic card to remark the position of the station lines.

27.
I finish the shaping of the hull using sandpaper blocks. This block has both a flat face and a rounded one. The paper is fitted using double sided tape, a major asset in any workshop. At this stage it is important to regularly check the dimensions of the hull. Using the templates, check the maximum breadth of the hull at each station line and the width at deck levels. Remember, of course, to take into account the thickness of the planking which is to be added later. Scrutinise the model carefully from all angles: your eye, possibly more than any calculations, will be a good judge to any emerging faults in the model's lines.

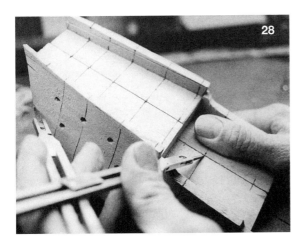

28.
A very important task is to establish the end of the counter. Measure up from the base line and back from the station lines. Then check, as illustrated in this photograph, the symmetry of both corners by measuring off from the same common reference point located amidships.

29.
Three templates prepared for the transom, the upper counter rail and the lower counter rail. These are used to mark in the correct curvature and distance above the base of the model of each of these features.

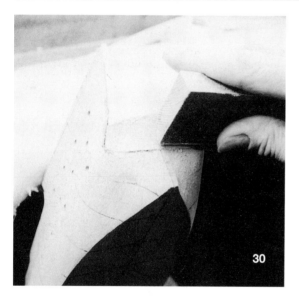

30.
The sanding block being used to shape the counter.

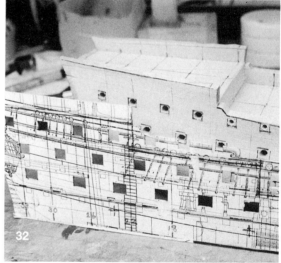

31.
The templates in use, with the smallest being used to precisely locate the transom.

32.
With a little manoeuvring, measuring and adapting to overcome the tumble-home, I have used the profile template to mark in the gunports and the tops of the bulwarks. The bulwarks are then cut down to the correct height, less the thickness of the capping rail. Note that, at this stage, I have included built up bulwarks for the poop. Soon after this I decided to fit an open rail and so it was cut down.

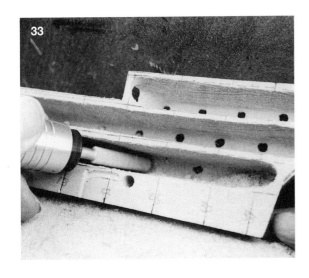

33.
Using a very course drum-shaped carbide cutter I am removing more wood from between the decks and thinning the broadside.

34.
With the sides thinned (see previous photograph) it is easy to trim the ports square with a sharp knife.

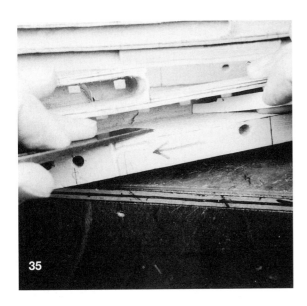

35.
Once more I have turned the blocks over and am levelling the decks using a chisel while employing a card jig to check the distance from the ports to the deck.

36.
The tops and undersides of the decks are then further tidied up with a sanding block.

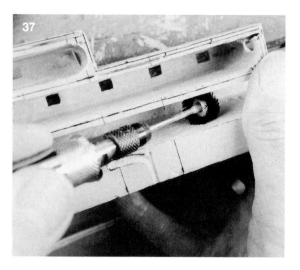

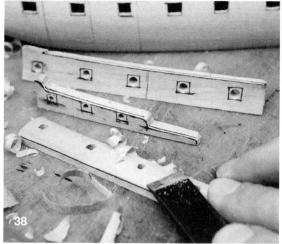

37.

Dust and burrs are being removed with a bristle brush on a rotary tool. This very handy gadget, much used by decoy duck carvers, is capable of putting an almost polished finish on wood.

38.

All the gunports have been cut out, although I shall return at a later stage to finally check and trim them. Now the bulwarks have been broken free (see No 24) and are being trimmed, thicknessed and shaped. The various sections will be between approximately ⅛ in and ¹⁄₁₆ in thick and particularly in the waist will taper noticeably towards the top. It is necessary to bear in mind the thickness of the planking when making these calculations.

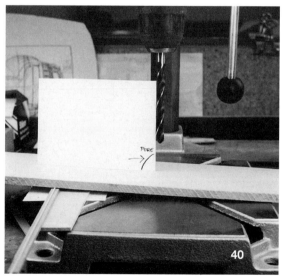

39.

The bulwarks, now at the correct thickness and with all their gunports cut out, have been returned to their positions although they have not yet been permanently fitted.

40.

The next job is to drill the hull to take the masts. As these are all set at different angles a drill press with an adjustable head is a boon. I, however, only have a very basic set-up so I am adjusting the angle by raising the stern by varying degrees for each mast. A card template for each mast is needed to set the angles.

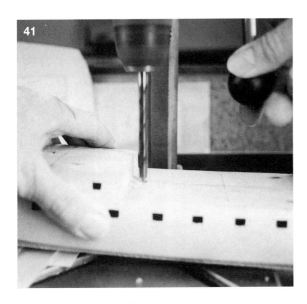

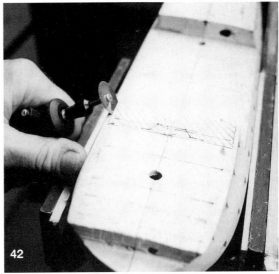

41.
The hull is being drilled. Make sure you set the drill press to drill just short of the base of the model.

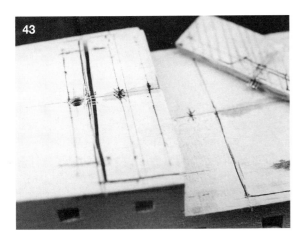

42.
Planked decks will eventually be fitted, so access to all those areas not enclosed by bulkheads will be required. First, I have marked in those areas of the deck to be removed so as to expose the deck below. I have then separated the two blocks and have used a thin cutting disk to cut slots along the edges of the decks, at the centreline on the inside of the face. This needs doing with care as the decks are by now quite thin. The slot should extend at least ¼in fore and aft of the thwartship lines which delineate the areas to be removed. I then carefully applied super-glue to the amidships deck edges, but only the edges of those sections to be removed. Care must be taken not to allow the glue to fill the slots. The two halves of the model are then pressed firmly together.

This done I am now removing the shaded area of deck using a very thin circular saw blade. Note the angle at which I am holding the saw. This is most important as it means that when the section of deck is refitted it will rest on the angled edge. To replace the wood removed by the saw cut, a strip of plane shaving is glued along the edges of the deck.

43.
Now the function of the slots becomes apparent. I have glued short lengths of brass wire into the ends of them. They now form dowels that will exactly relocate and hold the decks amidships, preventing any movement. (See No 148.)

44.
The hull showing the deck areas removed.

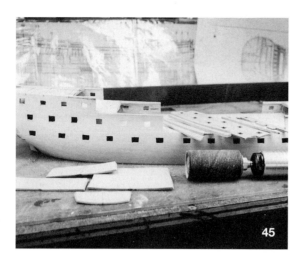

45.
All the inside edges of the bulwarks and the underside of all sections of the deck have been thinned. The rotary sander was the most useful tool for this work.

46.
Re-marking and final trimming to size of the gunports. Here a plastic jig is being used to check the dimensions of each port.

47.
Examination of this photograph will show that I have cut a rebate on either side of the hull to create a slot to accept the stem. This is then repeated aft for the stern-post. Also, using the home-made chisel in the pin vice, I have cut rebates to accept the knight-heads and finally have marked in, cut out and then finished with the round file, a hole to accept the bowsprit.

48.
Now to move on to the planking. Because many of the guns will need to be fitted before the two halves of the hull are finally glued together, it is advisable to finish the planking and the detail work on the broadsides first.

A card jig is being used to mark in the wales. This should be augmented with regular reference to the plans and, of course, as always, I constantly check by eye that all the lines run smoothly round the hull.

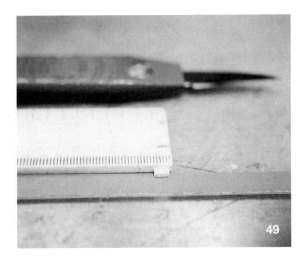

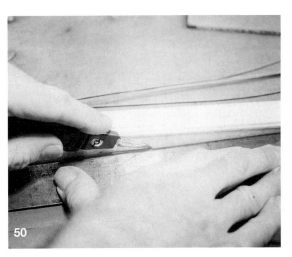

49.
I have prepared my planking from wood shavings glued to thin paper. These have received several coats of paint, with rubbing down between coats. This photograph shows one end of a white plastic ruler with a small rectangle of plastic card glued to its edge. The other end of the ruler is exactly the same. The thickness of the plastic card block represents the width of the planking to be cut. Pressed up against the ruler and under the blocks is a strip of shaving. A metal straight edge can now be moved towards the ruler until making contact with the plastic blocks.

50.
Then remove the ruler and make the cut.

52.
I decided to use anchor stock planking for the main wale, although after it was fitted and painted it was disappointingly subtle. It was, however, a very enjoyable process. I made this simple jig using two strips of brass angle and a couple of scraps of boxwood glued to a sheet of plywood as shown. The pieces of boxwood are the same distance apart as the length of the planks and the two brass sections are spaced to accept ten planks at a time.

51.
The wales have been glued in place and the planking is ready to be glued between them.

53.
The jig in use. Ten planks, cut to size and correctly thicknessed on the circular saw, are being shaped with a sharp chisel. They are then refitted the other way round and the process repeated.

54.
Planking the wale. As can be seen this method produces a very tight and neat fit between the planks. I must admit that, unfortunately, it worked rather too well. After painting it was almost impossible to make out the individual planks!

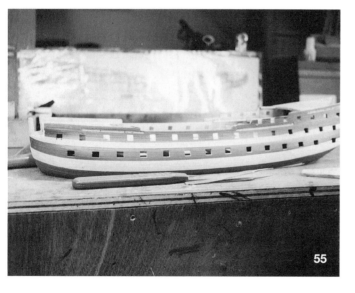

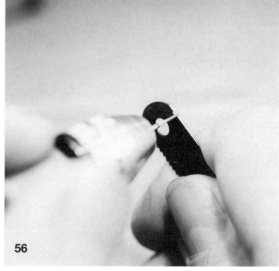

55.
Both of the wales and the rest of the planking is completed. Note that planks have been omitted where the channels are will be fitted. Note also that the painted planks do not follow the line of the gunports.

56.
There are a number of decorative rails to be fitted to the broadside. They can be built up from wire or, as I have chosen to do, be cut from boxwood. Here I am making a scraper from a piece of hacksaw blade, shaping it with a very fine diamond burr.

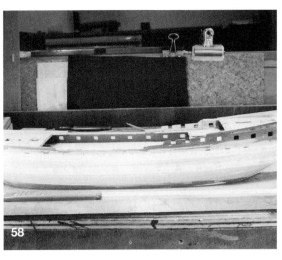

57.
Strips of boxwood have been prepared and are here being profiled using the scraper. They are then put on one side.

58.
I decided to complete the paint scheme on the hull at this stage, before fitting any of the relief detail. It would otherwise be difficult to fit the masking tape satisfactorily. The run of yellow bands is best achieved by applying a narrow strip of tape to delineate the top of each band and another for the bottom. Where there was any gap between them I applied a third strip. After applying the black paint, using an air brush, I removed the tape.

59.
Before fitting the mouldings a slot to receive the channels is being cut using a diamond burr.

60.
The moldings have now been fitted along the length of the hull and a fine diamond burr is being used to remove any sections crossing the ports.

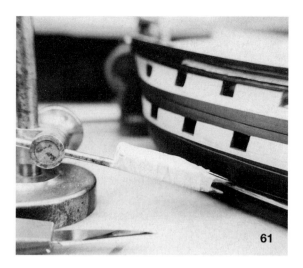

61.
After tidying up the black and ochre paint work, I am marking in the upper limit of the copper plating using a pencil taped to a gauge to ensure a straight line.

62.
Some tissue paper was given several coats of copper enamel followed by washes of green oil paint. This wash was prepared using artist's oil colours to represent the rich verdigris of weathered copper. Individual plates were cut from this sheet and are here being laid along the waterline.

63.
Using the knife to fair in the upper strake of copper. The plates are glued in place using Seccotine. The unwanted area below the knife cut can then be gently soaked and removed.

64.
The plating of the stern. When all the coppering is finished it is given another coat of green followed by a couple of diluted coats of a polyurethane 'Medium Oak' stained varnish. This gives a greater depth to the colour.

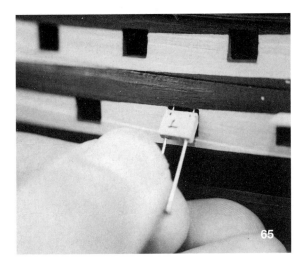

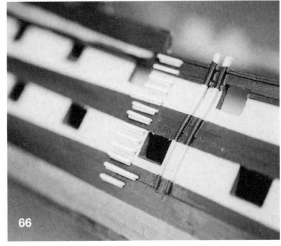

65.
This is not a gunport lid, but a jig made from a block of boxwood and two household pins. The aim is to mark the exact positions of the holes to be drilled which will take the gunport hinges. All the gunports fitted with lids are drilled at this stage.

66.
The chesstrees (not shown) and the fenders have been fitted and painted. I have just fitted the steps. Each is made up of two strips of wood which are easy to prepare and cut to length on the Preac saw. Before cutting off the individual lengths, the strips were sanded to their correct profile.

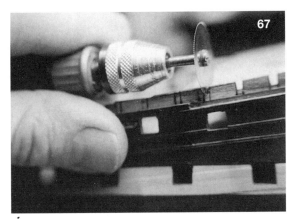

67.
I have marked in the positions for the stanchions supporting the quarterdeck rail and am here cutting out the apertures to receive them. These cuts will be finished with a sharp scalpel.

68.
The stanchions are fitted and their tops marked in.

69.
The stanchions are then trimmed with a sanding disk.

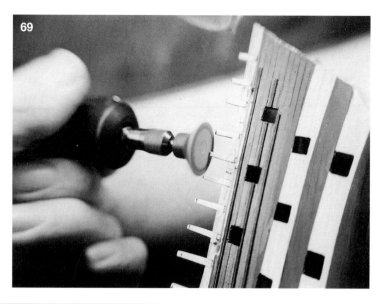

70.
The next job is to similarly fit the forecastle timberheads. I am shaping one here, on the end of a strip of boxwood, before cutting to length with the Preac saw.

Channels and Chainplates

71.
Having progressed so far with the hull, it's time to tackle the channels, chainplates and deadeyes. This photograph shows one of the channels being shaped.

72.
Here the timber heads and channels have all been glued into their pre-cut slots.

The completed model from the port bow.

The model from starboard. The cutter, with its crew, gives a good idea of the impressive size of a 74.

(Above) A close-up of cutter and crew.

(Below) This view of the stern shows clearly the carved decorative work and the two boats moored astern.

(Above) More details of the carvings. Also clearly shown are the main and mizzen chains beneath the channels, the lanterns and the tackles beneath the boom.

(Below) Looking down on the poop. Here are the carronades. This view also shows the quarter galleries well.

(*Above*) This view of the quarterdeck shows well some of the details beneath the break of the poop, but the wheel and binnacle are obscured by the ladder.

(*Below*) An overall view of the midship section of the model.

(Above) The seaman in the launch gives a good indication of the size of a 74's boats.

(Below) More figures help lend a sense of scale to the ship. The marine, just visible in the head, is dwarfed by the figurehead.

(Above) The starboard bow. Note in particular the fore topmast staysail in its 'hammock', the anchors, and the anchor buoy lashed to the shrouds.

(Below) The effectiveness of properly made and stained blocks is clearly demonstrated.

The ship from the starboard quarter.

73.
Once the channels are in place the inverted knee supports can be made and fitted. Enough rectangles of suitable timber have been cut to size and then each one has a corner removed on the saw. This will allow them to fit over the rail running immediately above the channel.

74.
Here the knees are being trimmed to shape with a scalpel. The removal of the corners, described in photograph 73, is clearly evident.

75.
After fitting, the knees can be finally shaped and finished. Here I am using a very fine ruby cutter.

76.
The making and fitting of curled ends to the moulded rails. I formed these from two different thicknesses of brass wire and glued one inside the other. One is shown on the left of the picture resting on the channel knees while another is shown fitted just to the right of the channel.

77.
This is a simple jig for forming eyebrows, each of which will be made of two separate pieces of wire. The upper ones are made first and then the jig is reshaped for the lower ones. These should be made of a slightly thinner wire and fit neatly inside the upper ones.

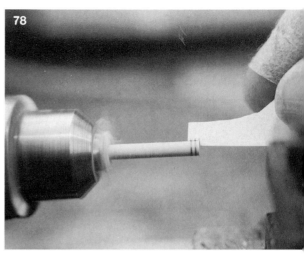

78.
Now for the deadeyes. I have put a strip of boxwood dowel into the chuck and turned it to the correct diameter. Using a plastic jig I have marked, with a pencil, the depth of the deadeye and the position of the groove for the strop.

79.
With a razor saw I have cut in the position of the groove and then, demonstrated here, a rather deeper one to form the deadeye.

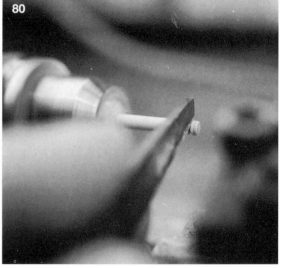

80.
This file has been ground down on the reverse side to form a knife-like edge and is here being used to shape the deadeye.

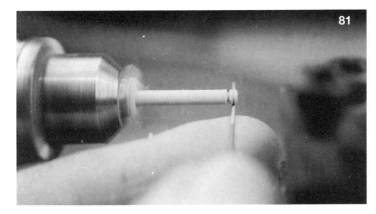

81.
A very fine round file being used to delineate the grove.

82.
A knife is used to finally detach the deadeye from the dowel.

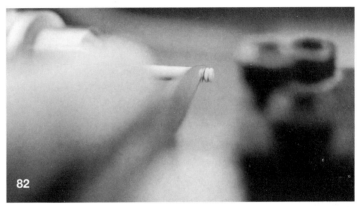

83.
Drilling a deadeye, using a drill made from an old drill shank. The tweezers have been shaped to fit the deadeye grooves.

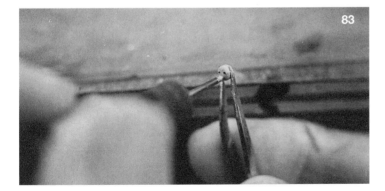

84.
After drilling, the top edges of the holes are recessed using the diamond burr.

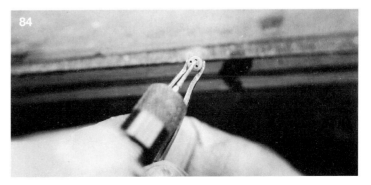

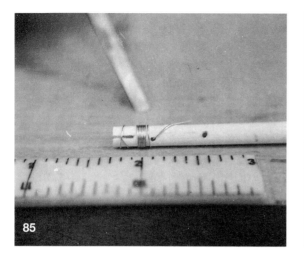

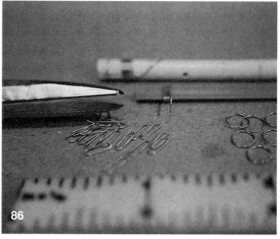

85.
The next long job is making up and fitting the chains.
I have made a boxwood jig to form the deadeye strops.
Trial and error will establish the correct diameters for
these jigs. The slot and holes enable the coils to be held
in place while the coils are cut through with a sharp
knife. For all these fittings I use a tinned copper wire.

86.
Here are two jigs, one round one and one made from
a flat plastic card for the middle chain. The scissors are
made from a hardened steel. If you look carefully you
will see how I have ground and sharpened the ends.
They cope easily with copper wire.

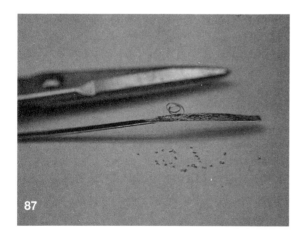

87.
A strip of silver solder beaten paper thin and then cut
into minute pieces, ready for joining the various com-
ponents of the chain-plates.

88.
I have linked middle and upper chain together, then
using a fine sable brush I have applied a touch of flux
to the two joins, followed by a piece of the silver solder.
The blow-torch is now being brought to bear on the
links, working in slowly from the side.

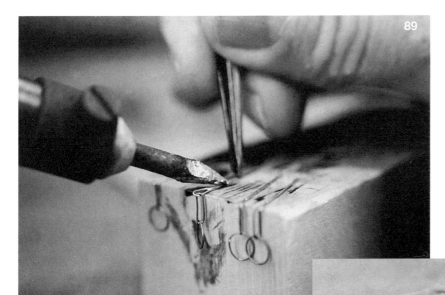

89.
Fitting the lower links. The lower half of these is soft soldered. This section will form the preventer plates.

90.
Deadeyes fitted in their chains.

91.
Before fitting the chains the position of the deadeyes and preventer plates are marked in using temporary masts and a length of string. Regular referral to the plans is, of course, essential.

92.
Deadeyes and chains glued in place. The diamond burr is being used to mark the position of the bolts.

93.
Drilling two holes in each of the preventer plates.

94.
Gluing and pinning the brass bolts in place using super-glue. The holes drilled for the port lid hinges can clear-ly be seen here.

95.
Trimming the pins flush with the plates. They will be finished off with a touch from a fine file.

96.
A simple but useful jig that, with various wedges, will hold the model securely while working on the ship's sides.

97.
The mizzen chains are not fitted with a long preventer plate, so I have drilled the hull and glued the lower chain directly into the hull. The small round plate and bolt will be suggested with a spot of white glue.

Decks and Armament

98.
Starting work on the guns. The first step is to chuck a length of dowel. Using the card jig, set this length about ⅛ in longer than the length of the barrel.

99.
The correct taper has been set and the barrel turned.

100.
Using another card jig make a cut with the razor saw to the length of the barrel and yet another cut to just beyond the end of the pommelion.

101.
Then remove the intervening wood and shape the pommelion.

102.
I mark the centre of the barrels with a point in the Minicraft drill before drilling the holes with a twist drill.

103.
Any further shaping can be carried out by fixing the barrel into a length of hollow plastic rod, slightly tapered on the inside, itself held in a drill.

104.
For the guns to be fitted below deck, in completely enclosed areas, I have constructed these simplified carriages. The front of the carriages and all that can be glimpsed through the port is to scale. They are painted and ready for fitting.

105.
Before fitting the cannon I mounted the half hull, on which I am going to work, onto this jig. It gives easy viewing and good lighting to internal and external areas.

106.
I have used boxwood sheet to form strips of shaped decking along the sides of the deck. These were held temporarily in place using some 'sprung' plastic card wedges. The guns were then mounted using woodworkers' glue.

107.
Each gun is checked carefully for position from the outside of the hull. When the glue is dry, guns and decking are removed.

108.
Before finally fitting the guns, the port lids have to be made and fitted. These are cut from boxwood and drilled and fitted with false hinges. The same jig that was used to drill the holes above the ports is used to position the hinges. Here is a port lid being held by these wire false hinges. Scale paper hinges have been fitted and holes drilled to take the ringbolts. These are made from tinned copper wire formed round a drill shank, trimmed and here glued in place.

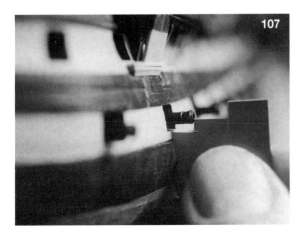

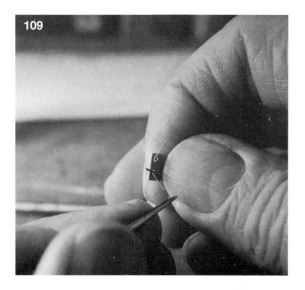

109.
The other end of the wire is here being shaped round the drill shank to form a ringbolt on the underside of the lid. When all the lids are thus detailed they can be fitted to the hull.

110.
The lids being fitted. Short sections of boxwood dowel have been cut and fitted to form the hinge barrels. Holes have been drilled in the hull for the lifting ropes and these are now being fitted. They are made from pre-painted wire. The hooked end, being held in the tweezers, will be fitted round the ring before squeezing the two ends together, touching with a spot of glue and repainting.

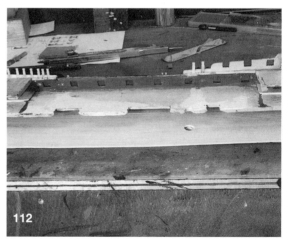

111.
One of the reasons for mounting the guns, in the way I have, will now become clearer. I can think of nothing more frustrating than an accidental blow to a gun barrel causing it to break loose and become irretrievably lost below decks. As can be seen here, I have drilled and am doweling down through barrel, carriage and deck before refitting the strips of deck in exactly the same way as done previously; only this time gluing in place with Araldite.

112.
This photograph portrays the process of fitting a section of pre-lined decking over the central section of the lower deck. Perhaps this is unnecessary but this deck may just be visible later through open hatches beneath the boats. (Also see No 135.)

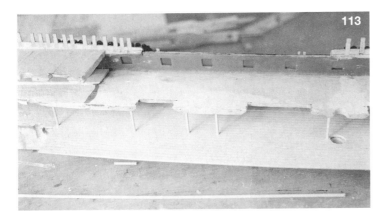

113.
Pillars are just being fitted to strengthen and give support to the upper deck. When they, and the two lengths of threaded stainless steel rod, are in place the two halves of the hull can finally be glued together.

114.
Now the model has been mounted on a temporary base consisting of a plank with two side pieces. This allows the rods to pass through the base and be secured with nuts underneath.

115.
Work on the upper deck is started next. Here the decking is being prepared. Before cutting the individual planks from the mounted wood shavings I gave them two coats of clear French polish. This soaks in and prevents the glue from staining the wood whilst the planks are being laid. I had added a small amount of 'raw umber' watercolour to the Seccotine in order to suggest the dark caulking. When the deck is finished it can finally be wiped over with a small amount of methylated spirit to remove any shine. The finished decking can be placed under pressure until needed.

116.
Now to the guns. This is where my small saw really comes into its own. Although I have some very fine saw blades I have not, so far, needed to fit them. The comparatively coarse blade, seen here, produces almost polished cuts. Here I have prepared a strip of holly, *cut across the grain*, and profiled it on the saw. The curve in the base will now be rounded off with a round file.

117.
Here are the individual sides for the carriages being sliced off.

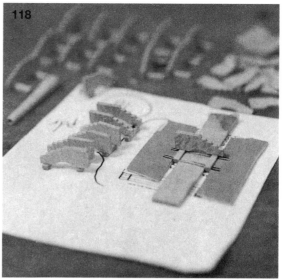

118.
This simple jig was made to position the two axletrees at the correct distance apart. It consists of three strips of wood glued to the square of card. I am fitting the axeltrees directly beneath the sides and at this stage they can be made over length.

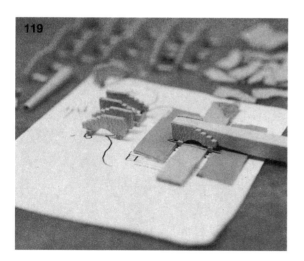

119.
A simple spacer is being used to check the converging angle and the distance apart of the sides.

120.
After fitting the transom and bolster the ends of the axletrees are being sanded flush with the sides.

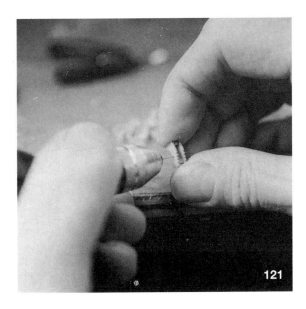

121.
Drilling for the long bolt that joins the two sides and will support the bed for the quoin.

122.
Bolts fitted.

123.
The ends of the axletrees are being drilled, at a central point where they join the side, ready to receive the dowel that will form the rounded end of the axletree.

124.
Turning the wheels for the guns. The same procedure is used as was employed for the deadeyes (see Nos 78-83). The only real difference concerns the drilling of each wheel with the bit mounted in the tailstock.

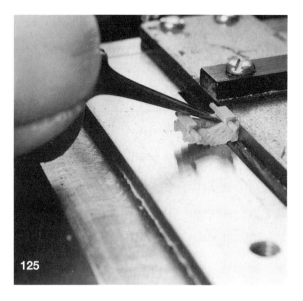

125.
Short lengths of boxwood dowel have been glued in the holes drilled for them and the carriage is now being run over the saw blade to establish the grooves for the trunnions.

126.
These grooves are now finished with a diamond burr.

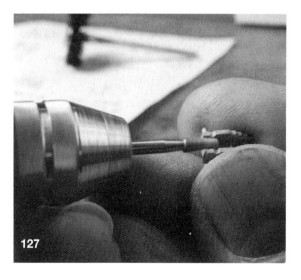

127.
A slightly larger burr is being used to finish shaping the transom.

128.
Carriages, wheels and barrels.

129.
The next job is to produce the required number of eyebolts for both the carriages and the ship's side. A lot of these are required and the easiest and best way to paint them is to mount them in a strip of Plasticene and then use an airbrush.

130.
This simple boxwood jig is used while drilling the holes for the eyebolts. It locates over the axles and has holes pre-drilled to give the correct position for the eyebolts.

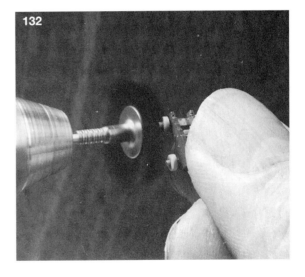

131.
After painting the carriages and the inner faces of the wheels, the latter are glued in place on their axles which can then be sanded to the correct length.

132.
A touch with the bristle brush removes any burrs left by the sanding, leaving the carriage ready for the painting and for the fitting of the eyebolts.

133.
A painted carriage with wheels and eyebolts fitted.

134.
Before returning to work on the hull it is a good idea to screw a couple of planks either side of the base to protect the work done on the broadside before moving on to the decks.

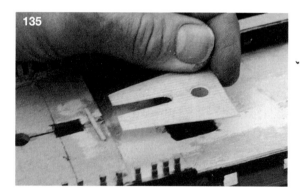

135.
Whoops! Before fitting the two halves together I should have planked the areas of the upper deck beneath the openings for ladders on the forecastle and quarterdeck. I didn't! I now had to make up sections of decking to be inserted beneath these decks in the relevant positions. This one can just be manoeuvred into place under the forecastle. It fits between the two boxwood planks on which the guns are mounted and has a hole cut for the foremast and a slot removed to accommodate the bowsprit. After fitting these I prepared a card template from which to cut the decking for the upper deck. I measured and cut this template as accurately as possible. However, if (and there is always an 'if') the edges do not match the insides of the bulwarks exactly, I stick other small pieces of card on top of the template until it fits tight to the bulwarks and I am satisfied. This template is used to mark out the deck on a sheet of prepared decking and this is then cut to size and any openings marked in pencil. It is glued in place using an impact adhesive.

136.
Before proceeding further, gratings need to be made. The whole process is clearly explained by Nepean Longridge in his now classic work *The Anatomy of Nelson's Ships*. Using the Preac saw this method proved to be very straightforward. A 20 thou. saw blade was used and a boxwood sheet slotted and fitted to the saw table using some double-sided tape. A 20 thou. square guide was glued 20 thou. away from the saw blade. The photograph illustrates this clearly and also shows a strip of boxwood being prepared by simply running the wood over the saw, locating each preceding cut over the guide.

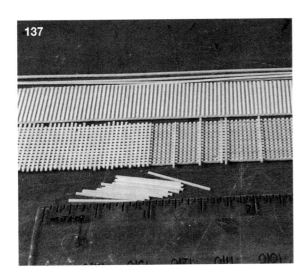

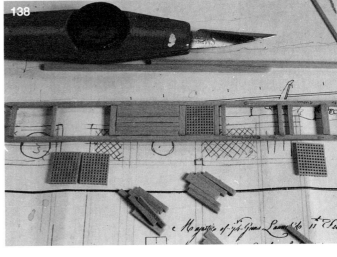

137.
The saw is then reset and 20 thou. strips cut from the stock. At the same time some 20 thou. square material is prepared and cut into suitable lengths. Here a strip of grating is being assembled. This job can be a little tricky. It helps to use double-sided tape to hold the ends of the long strips in place, and to continually check the distance between them using 20 thou. spacers. Before fitting each strip I have run a little white woodworking glue along its underside. When completed the grating needs rubbing down and once more the rotary brush is used to polish and de-burr. This little tool really works miracles here, cleaning up all the edges of the timbers . . . in a matter of seconds!

138.
The hatches for the upper deck can now be assembled. I like to cut all gratings to size first and build the frames around them. This ensures a perfect fit.

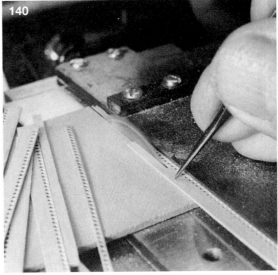

140.
Strips of timber are then sliced from this stock before being finally trimmed to size. Identical blanks are cut for the bottoms.

139.
Here the Unimat is being employed to prepare a strip of boxwood for the shot racks that will run either side of the hatches. The distance between each hole is determined by the number of turns or part turns given to the hand wheel.

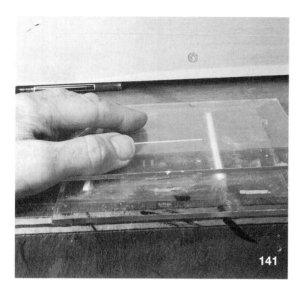

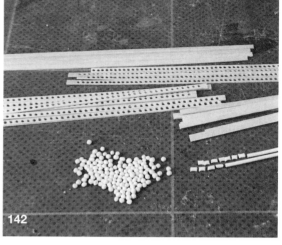

141.

Manufacturing cannon balls at a small scale is always a problem, especially if you want them exactly the right size. This is the method I use, which was shown to me by a friend. The photograph shows two sheets of glass. Two plastic strips have been glued onto the lower one. The area between them has been lightly coated with talcum powder. By moving the top sheet of glass gently back and forth over the strips, a rod has been formed from a piece of Milliput (the horizontal line apparently emanating from the end of my thumb).

142.

In the foreground are two rods of Milliput. They have been allowed to set slightly before being cut into even lengths which are then rolled between the tips of thumb and forefinger to form the finished balls. Behind these are prepared strips for both the 18- and 9 pdr shot racks.

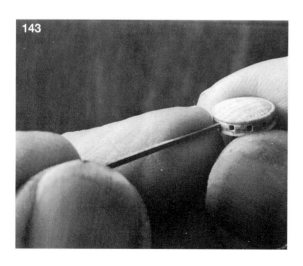

143.

Two capstans are required. The barrels and drumheads have been turned on the lathe from one piece of holly and holes have been drilled for the bars. These are being squared with a small file.

144.

Whelps and cheeks are next cut and fitted in this manner . . .

145.
. . . before shaping the capstan, firstly with a diamond burr and . . .

146.
. . . then with a suitable file.

147.
A finished capstan and hatch coaming. The far opening will house a grating, but the one next to the capstan will be fitted with a ladder to the lower deck. It has, therefore, been fitted with boxwood sides to cover the original wood deck. These sides are glued to the hatch coaming. The whole unit is still removable as is the forward bulkhead which is being assembled behind it.

148.
The bulkhead has had further detail added using strips of thin card. Showing clearly are the ends of the slots cut in the deck edges before the two halves of the model were assembled and into which the brass dowels in the edge of the removable section of deck will locate.

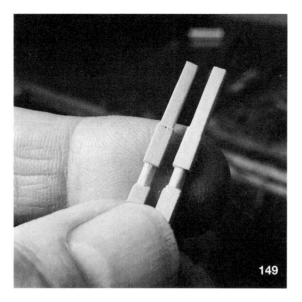

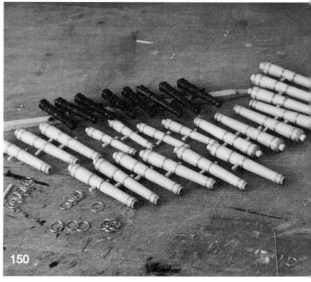

149.

The next job is the detailing of the upper deck. Here the two uprights for the gallows bits have been hand carved. The round sections will locate in the holes drilled in the decks.

150.

Now to complete the barrels for the guns. They have been drilled and fitted with boxwood trunnions. The rings have been prepared by winding wire around various sizes of drill shanks and they are then super-glued in place, with the join located underneath the barrel.

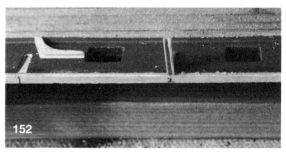

151.

The completed barrels - some of which are mounted in their carriages.

152.

Before proceeding to fit the upper deck guns, it is a good idea to think ahead to the installation of the gangways. I think it is likely that, at this date, these would have been supported by wooden knees fitted with iron brackets for the skid beams. For the model the brackets will partly be simulated using strips of paper but, for the sake of strength, I intend making the main supporting bar from piano wire. (See Nos 162-164.) This will become clear in later photographs, but for the moment I have made the knees, the tops of which have been slotted on the Preac saw, to accept the wire and have cut tenons in the bulwarks in which to locate the knees. They are then numbered and put on one side.

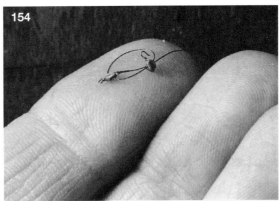

153.
Preparing blocks for the gun tackles. I will give a detailed description of the methods I am employing for block making when I reach the running rigging, as it will be clearer and easier to photograph when working on some of the larger blocks. (See Nos 340-345.) Suffice to say that several options are open to the miniaturist and much depends on the scale of the model. At ³⁄₃₂ in - 1ft there is no reason why the blocks cannot be carved from boxwood, be stained and then stropped with either wire or thread. They really do look so much better than simulated ones. However, the job is seriously time-consuming!

154.
A very fine needle has been used to open the strop on the single block sufficiently to allow the thread to pass through. The thread is then secured with a half hitch and the remaining end is glued to the main rope with a touch of super-glue. When all the tackles have been prepared in this way and the bulwarks drilled and fitted with the requisite eyebolts, the guns can be fitted and tackles rigged.

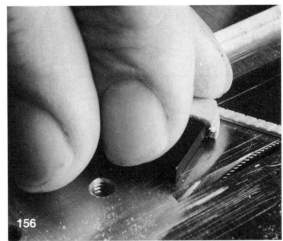

155.
There are various ways of constructing ladders. Working to this scale, I have chosen to adhere as closely as possible to full-size practice. After preparing stock for both the sides and treads I have set the cross cut guide to the required angle, marked in the position of the treads on one of the strips prepared for the sides, and am here cutting groves in the underside. Care has to be taken to line up the saw blade with the pencil marks, checking the accuracy directly from above.

156.
The grooved strip has been turned over and fixed to the opposing one with double-sided tape. This time I lined up the original saw cuts with the saw blade to produce the twin of the original strip. Sections can now be cut from these two strips to form the sides of each ladder.

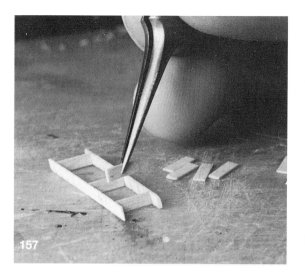

157.
When assembling a ladder, one rung is glued in place at either end before slotting the others into place and securing with a touch of glue.

158.
The large double ladder down to the lower gundeck was first made up as a wide single one and then, as is shown in this photograph, run over the saw blade to cut half way through the treads.

159.
A narrow strip of boxwood is then glued into the grooves in the treads to form the central runner. An extra scrap of wood is fitted at the top to complete the ladder.

160.
The ladders have been stained, painted and fitted along with iron stanchions and rope handrails. The shot racks are in place and ringbolts fitted for the train tackles. Various coils of rope have been formed and glued down and a length of cable ranged along the deck.

161.
Another photograph of the deck at this stage with the 18pdrs rigged and the knees for the gangways glued in place. Also fitted is the inboard end of the fore sheet.

162.
A diamond burr being used to extend the slots for the piano wire out to the ship's side.

163.
The forward end of the quarterdeck is curved, so extra sections are cut from jelutong and fitted at this stage. Note that these sections are relieved at their ends to take the gangways and that the sides of the deck are higher than the sheer. By the end of the eighteenth century the gangways would almost certainly have been raised to the level of the forecastle and quarterdeck thus necessitating the raising of the sheer. This will be accomplished on the model with a strip of boxwood, but, only after fitting the wire brackets and gangways. This will effectively lock the brackets in place. The raised area will finally be planked over in keeping with the rest of the ship's side.

164.
The piano wire brackets in place.

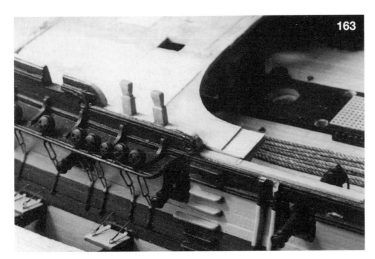

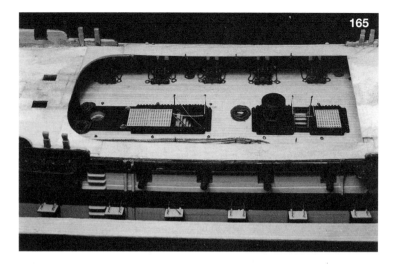

165.
Strips of thin plywood, that will form the under deck for the gangways, have been fitted port and starboard but, like the remainder of the deck, they have not yet been planked.

166.
A card template being prepared for the forecastle deck. A thin strip has been glued along its edge to give a good fit to the bulwarks. A similar one is made for the quarterdeck. Using the templates both decks are then cut from the pre-prepared decking and glued down with an impact adhesive. I prefer 'Thix-o-fix' for this job as it allows for some alignment before finally bedding down.

167.
The next job is to fit margin planks at the break of the forecastle and quarterdecks and then to plank the gangways. Using the Preac saw I cut some thin planks of yellow cedar for this job. The straight margin plank for the forecastle is straightforward, as is the gangway planking. The curved edge to the quarterdeck, however, is not quite so simple. I have to trim away all the decking material from the edge of the deck, and in order to do this I have made up this simple tool. A scalpel blade has been driven through a scrap of wood and another rounded piece of wood has been glued underneath it.

168.
The tool in use. Several light passes work better than applying too much pressure.

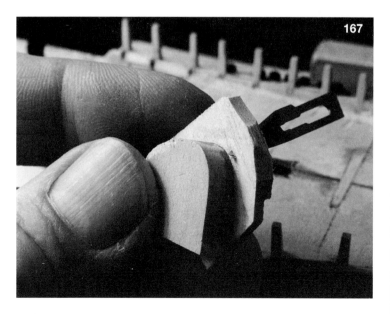

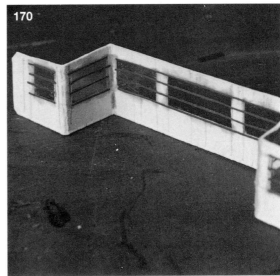

169.
The edge of the false deck has been faced with a strip of painted shaving and the first section of margin plank has been cut and fitted in place. It will not be trimmed to size until the remaining planks have been fitted. I determine the shape of each plank by laying a small piece of carbon paper, right side up, over the section of deck edge to be planked. The margin plank is then laid over this and burnished with a suitable tool thereby transferring the line of the edge of the planking to the underside of the margin plank. This can then be accurately trimmed to shape and fitted.

170.
The bulkhead of the poop is one of those features that involves quite a lot of work yet will hardly be conspicuous on the finished model. This is particularly so on *Majestic* where it is set back even further than on many other 74s. The first stage is to build a card frame and ensure a good fit – either side and top and bottom. Here the glazed areas have been removed and windows of acetate have been cut and fitted. Horizontal glazing bars, cut from pre-painted paper, have been glued in place.

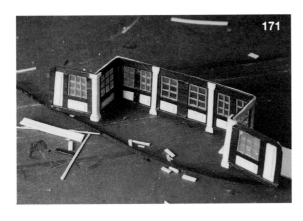

171.
The exterior detailing of the bulkhead. The main upright sections were the first to be fitted, along with the vertical glazing bars. These can then be trimmed before fitting the horizontal framing. Work has also been started on the decorative columns.

172.
A wheel, binnacle and two of the 9pdr guns have to be installed before the forward end of the poop is fitted. Here the framework for the binnacle has been prepared. The end sections will be trimmed to the marking shown. This will leave four extensions to the legs that will be glued into holes drilled in the deck. Either side will be faced with acetate after detailing the interior.

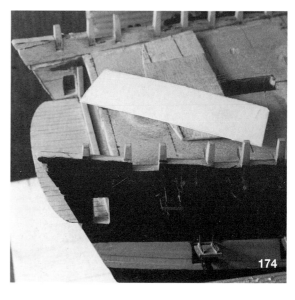

173.
The finished bulkhead in place along with the wheel and binnacle. This has been panelled with stained wood shavings. A brass lantern and pipe were turned and two small compasses made which are just visible.

174.
Next, the screen bulkhead is cut from card and some boxwood strip fitted, either side and across the deck below, against which the bulkhead will be located.

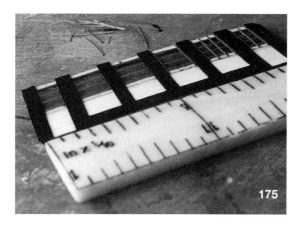

175.
Detailing the bulkhead.

176.
Completed and fitted. Note the small door to the quarter gallery and the panelling port and starboard.

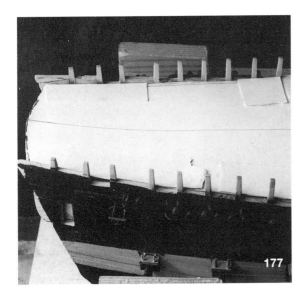

177.
The sections at either end of the poop deck, earlier removed, have been glued in place and a card template is being prepared for the planking.

178
The planked deck fitted.

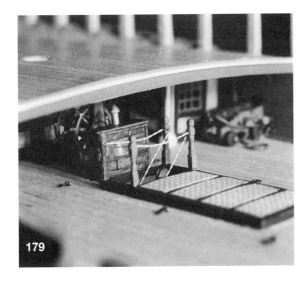

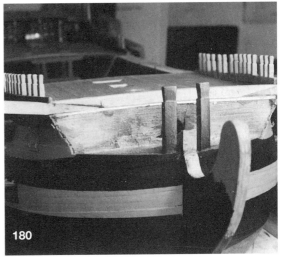

179.
The edge of the poop deck has been faced and the margin plank is in place. The turned stanchions and rope handrails for the ladder down to the upper deck have just been fitted, but I wish I had done this job before fitting the overhanging deck.

180.
The catheads are made in three sections. The end sections need careful shaping as they angle forwards and upwards. After fitting them the centre section, curved to the camber of the deck, is mitred and doweled in place over them.

181.
Bitts and panels are fitted to the front of the forecastle.

182.
The next job is the fitting of the plank sheer and fiferail. Both can be seen here temporarily fitted together with double sided tape. The positions of the bitts have been marked and they have been drilled with a fine drill.

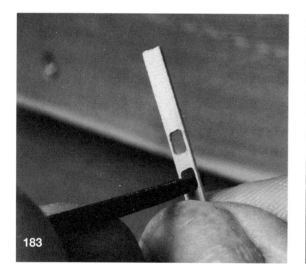

183.
After opening further with a fine diamond burr, each hole is finished with a file, checking all the time that the rail fits over all the bitts along its whole length.

184.
The plank sheer has been fitted and the fiferail is being glued in place. A boxwood spacer is being used to position it correctly at each bitt.

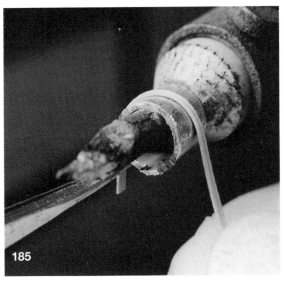

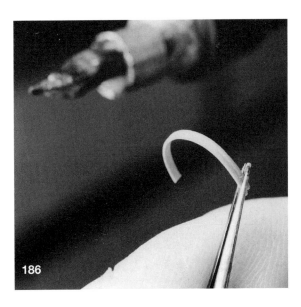

185.
Both roundhouses were shaped from turned jelutong dowel and glued in place. Their planking was very straightforward apart from the two bands of curved moulding needed for each. These were formed, as shown, around a strip of aluminium tube heated on a soldering iron.

186.
When removed from the heat the boxwood moulding should retain its shape.

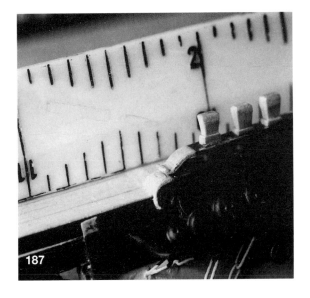

187.
Any curved sections of rail are also shaped using this method.

188.
Here, the same processes are being applied to the poop.

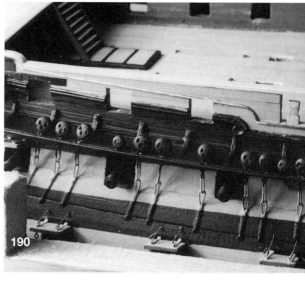

189.
I decided that by the end of the eighteenth century there was a strong likelihood that the quarterdeck bulwarks would have been built up, in a similar manner to those on the *Victory*. Some rebuilding work was, therefore, undertaken. Here, a section of brass rod is being made into a half-round section for decorative rails.

190.
The bulwarks being reconstructed and fitted with the new rails.

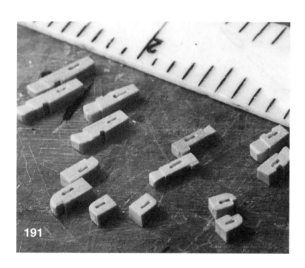

191.
A number of belaying kevels will be required. They are made from boxwood, drilled and then relieved with a fine diamond burr to suggest the sheaveholes.

192.
The same method used to form the sheaveholes in the cathead.

193.
A ⅛in thick rectangle of clear polystyrene was used as the basis around which to construct the poop skylight. Here three of the sides have been fitted. All the woodwork was done with boxwood cut to size on the circular saw.

194.
The hole in the poop has been carefully trimmed to accept the skylight and a rail is being fitted at deck level.

195.
The glazing bars being fitted.

196.
Some two-ply yellow cedar, made from plane shavings, has been prepared for the quarterdeck rail. Due to the curved deck edge it needs to be quite large.

197.
The 'ply' is held in place and marked from below to the curve of the deck with a section of 0.3mm pencil lead fitted into a scrap of wood.

198.
Two rails are required. When cut from the 'ply' they have to be joined, both to one another, and to the deck edge with small pieces of double-sided tape before being drilled for the stanchions.

199.
Square blocks of boxwood have been cut and drilled and a length of brass rod fitted to each one as the basis for each of the stanchions.

200.
The rails have been fitted over the brass rods, the tops trimmed and sanded flush, the centres have been built up with PVA glue and the whole structure removed, painted and then refitted.

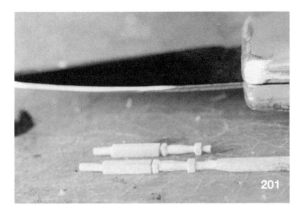

The Belfry

201.
The belfry is a very prominent deck fitting so some care should be taken in its construction. This photograph shows two of the uprights — a completed one and, in the foreground, one trimmed to size using a craft knife. After cutting away from the stock it will be finished with a fine file whilst mounted in the drill chuck.

202.
The two sides of the belfry assembled.

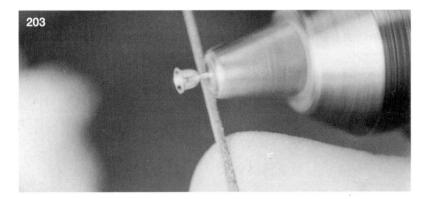

203.
The bell was turned in the chuck of the Minicraft drill, first with a diamond burr mounted in another drill, and then with a very fine file.

204.
The base of the belfry with its bell fitted. On the right can be seen two wood shavings being super-glued together over a drill bit to form the curved 'ply' used for the top of the belfry.

205.

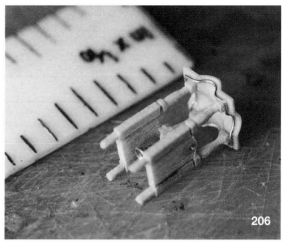

206.

205.
The top of the belfry being assembled from the curved 'ply', formed around the drill bit.

206.
The completed belfry. Four squares of wood were added to the top as corners before trimming all to size and fitting to the base. Finally, a 'beading' of wire was glued under the top.

207

208

The Stern

207.
Constructing a stern for one of these vessels is always a challenging job. The important thing to strive for is the creation of graceful curves and sweeping lines, while integrating the carvings and decoration so that they become a part of the structure rather than an added afterthought. So often otherwise superb models are spoilt by awkward carvings. Working to a small scale like this I tend to see the whole job as a piece of sculpture, as much as a technical exercise. It is necessary to continually check the stern from all angles by eye and if anything looks wrong, move and rebuild until satisfied – if ever that's possible! It helps to have a vice available while doing this work, so that the model can be set at the best angle for the job.

208.
I am making a start on the lower bank of windows. The material used is 0.5mm ply. After marking out the windows they are opened by drilling and then trimming with a craft knife.

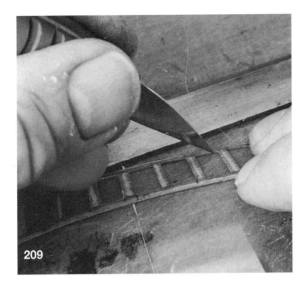

209.
Using the ply strip as a guide the individual windows are being cut from acetate.

210.
The windows are glued in place along with the horizontal glazing bars and some of the framing. This is cut from thin card.

211.
The basic structure for the quarter galleries is based on three blocks of wood per side. They are very roughly shaped, then fitted in place with double-sided tape, marked, removed, re-trimmed and refitted. This exercise is carried out as many times as proves necessary. When reasonably satisfied that they are correctly shaped they are hollowed out where required. They are then glued permanently to the hull before final finishing. This photograph shows the lower block at an early stage of shaping.

212.
Work is progressing on all three quarter galleries.

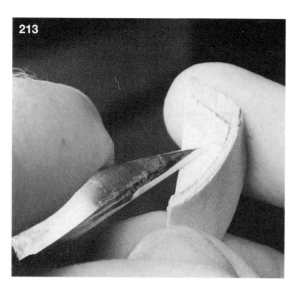

213.
Hollowing out a quarter gallery

214.
The lower two have been finished, but the top one is still over size.

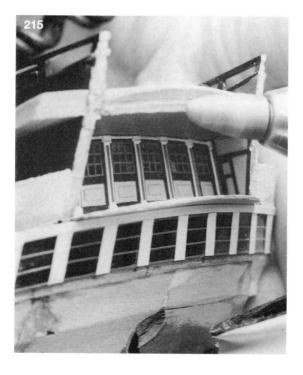

215.
Cutting in the arch above the gallery. A strip of quarter round material has been fitted over the end of the poop planking and is here being hollowed out from below.

216.
The upper section of the stern has been cut from ply and the windows for the upper quarter galleries fitted. At this stage, on refitting this section to the model, the windows were found to be a fraction too high so a rectangle encompassing the window has been cut out and a strip re-inserted at the top. This task does illustrate just one of the ways in which things can be moved around and changed.

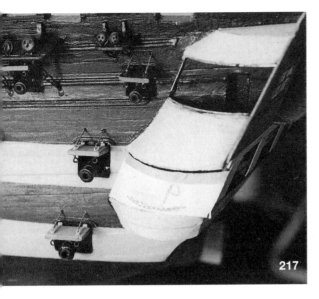

217.
Brass wire frames have been fitted around the areas to be 'glazed'. They are set slightly back. A card template is being cut and fitted to the lower ones.

218.
Acetate 'windows' fitted. They have been glued to the wire frames at top, bottom and at either end and are now flush with the wooden sections.

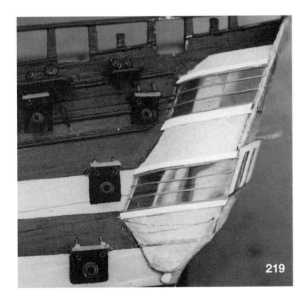

219.
Horizontal glazing bars and the commencment of the framing.

220.
Verticals fitted but not yet trimmed to length. All this work is carried out using thin card. I prefer a good quality Bristol board.

221.
This section of junior hacksaw blade has been notched using a diamond burr. It has then been used to produce the moulded edge on the boxwood plank it is resting on. The edge will be run off on the saw and used to form the various rails around the stern and quarter galleries. They will be given the correct curvature before fitting using the method outlined in photographs 185 and 186.

222.
Rails have been cut, shaped and fitted to the quarter galleries.

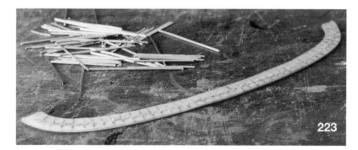

223.
Before going any further, I have turned my attention to the handrail around the gallery, as I want the ends to blend in smoothly with the rails. This photograph depicts the base for the rail. When in place it will overhang the planked deck by approximately two thirds of its width. It has been drilled to accept the bases of the balusters. These have been cut from brass rod.

224.
The base of the rail temporarily fitted in place and a brass rod, that will form part of the top rail, has been shaped and temporarily fitted in two holes in the quarter galleries.

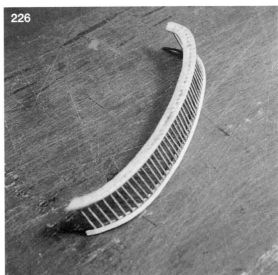

225.
Each of the balusters has been inserted through the holes in the base rail and their tops super-glued to the top brass rail. A narrow card strip is now glued around the top edges. More glue will then be run in from above.

226.
The whole structure has been removed and is seen here from below, the ends of the balusters that extended below the base rail have been trimmed and filed flush.

227.
Now some quite fine work is required. The railing has been fixed in place on a block of wood. The knife and narrow strip of card are used to cut the small squares that will form the tops and bottoms of the balusters. These will need to be angled as the sides are approached. The middle of the balusters are built up using the glue.

228.
The balusters formed.

229.
Permanently fitted. A ply capping rail has now been added and a brass rail fitted beneath the base.

230.
Now the remaining rails can be fitted and the pilasters built up from card and paper. Note how the rails follow round the stern and blend with the handrail around the gallery.

231.
A wire rail has been fitted beneath the upper gallery rim and above the middle stool rail to which have been glued the wire balusters. They are in the process of being built up with the PVA glue.

232.
The transom and counter have been planked and I am now moving on to the upper stern. Before starting on the carvings I have fitted the necking of the taffrail. This photograph, looking from below, shows this feature fairly clearly. It has been formed from a strip of paper, tapered at either end. This has been glued in place above the cove, forming a projecting shelf. It is finished with a length of twisted wire. The same process has been used to form the projecting arches over the stern windows to the quarter galleries.

233.
Now on to the carvings. I chose to sculpt these from Milliput. In the past I always started by building an armature of wire and wood that is then progressively built up with PVA adhesive and artist's gesso. At this slightly larger scale I felt that the direct sculpting method was more appropriate. I started with a thick sausage for the torso, thinner ones for arms and legs as well as a round blob for the head. These were then shaped into what was, a reasonable semblance of a human figure using a variety of tools. The figure was allowed to harden a little before adding the drapes from thin strips of Milliput.

234.
The drapes can be seen being applied and shaped using a home-made boxwood tool. Again, they were then left to harden. When the figures and other carvings were completely cured I reworked them, adding detail, smoothing and undercutting using a fine diamond burr. I tried to slant the shoulders and hips of the figures, introducing as much movement and life as possible, further emphasising these lines using the draperies and other carvings. The end result, I'm afraid, is still a poor reflection of the wonderful contemporary carvings found on some of the Navy Board models of this period.

The decorative work found on the ships, or at least on the contemporary ship models, of this period was still strongly influenced by the highly decorative and curvilinear Baroque style of earlier years. Although the profusion of carvings and painted decoration was severely limited after the restrictive order of 1703, the Georgian style of carving, as found on the larger warships of this period, was still characterised by curves and flowing lines.

235.
The carvings completed. A wire rim has been added to the coats of arms. They will not be finally painted until I'm ready to paint those for the stem. The taffrail rail can also be seen being fitted in sections.

236.
The view from inboard showing three boxwood knees cut and fitted.

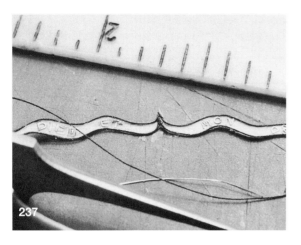

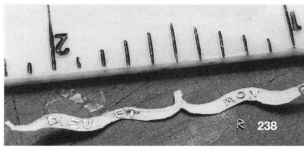

238.
The edging is next built up with a fine thread, again using super-glue. When dry the edges are sanded and the whole scroll given a couple of coats of dark blue paint before the border and the letters are picked out in gold.

237.
A feature of the arch above the gallery is the scroll carrying the Prince of Wales's motto. The scroll was cut from paper and the letters formed from fine copper wire that had been slightly flattened with a small hammer. The letters are here being glued in place with super-glue.

240.
The tops of the quarter galleries have been finished with copper shingles punched from the same tissue paper as was used for the hull coppering.

The upper finishing is fitted above this. I made this from a strip of brass etched material previously intended for the barred front of a chicken coup. It has been fitted top and bottom with boxwood rails. Apart from some touching up of the paint work, this completes the work on the stern.

239.
The scroll fitted, and the lower finishing and the drop, located beneath the quarter galleries, have been decorated, again using strips of Milliput. The remaining sections of taffrail rail have been fitted and the rail continued across the stern. The curves were set using the soldering iron and copper tube. It was made in three sections.

Contemporary paintings of ships of this period give the impression that most of the decorative carvings were gilded, or gilt painted. The more likely finish would have been varnish applied over a white paint to give the impression of gilt. This is the treatment I have chosen for the mass of the carvings on the stern, although touches of gold will be used on the coats of arms for instance. I wanted a fairly subdued finish so used a natural wood colour rather than white and used a medium oak stained varnish over this. It was applied fairly liberally to allow it to run into recesses and folds, so highlighting the raised features. Several coats were applied.

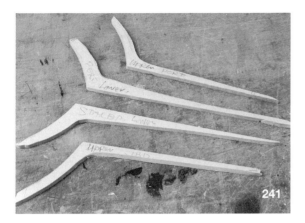

The Bow and Figurehead

241.
Now for some of the tricky bits. The complex arrangements of rails and brackets that make up the graceful lines leading up to the figurehead deserves great care and attention. The lines should be smooth and symmetrical but it is not easy to achieve as there is hardly a straight line to be found. This is my method. I do a lot of measuring and checking using dividers and callipers but in the end depend more on 'eye' than anything else. This photograph shows the upper and lower cheeks, roughly cut to size from holly. I sometimes use boxwood but find that holly takes a curve rather better.

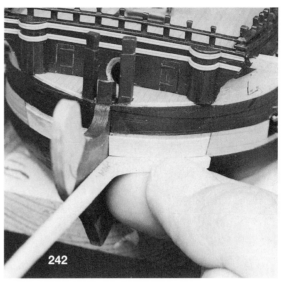

242.
The filling pieces have been cut and glued to the hull and the lower cheek is being offered up to the hull to check for fit.

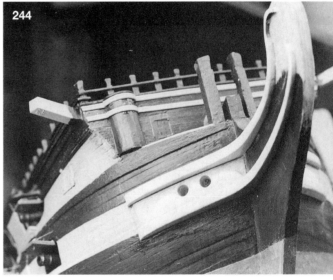

244.
Upper and lower cheeks glued in place.

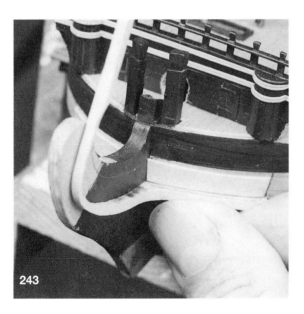

243.
The lower cheek, curved, using the technique outlined in Nos 185-186, is being checked for fit against the stem.

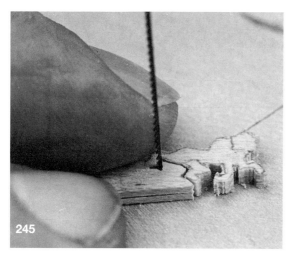

245.

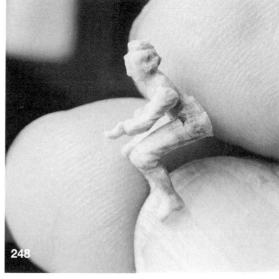

246.

245.
Before going any further with the rails I am breaking off to make and fit the figurehead and related carvings, and apply the scrolls between the cheeks. Two thin sheets of holly have been fixed together with double-sided tape before using a fine vibrating fret saw to cut out both silhouettes of the lions.

246.
The odds and ends of King George are cut in a similar manner. The arms and legs are separate from the head/torso section, which I have already started shaping with the diamond burrs.

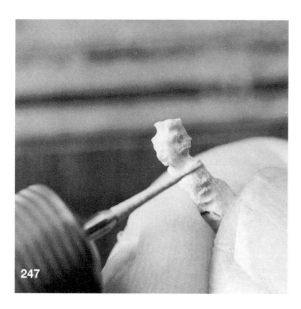

247.

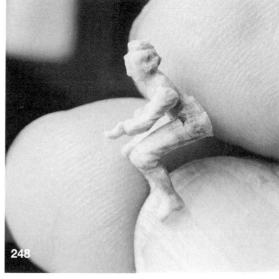

248.

247.
Further shaping of the torso.

248.
Arms and legs have been carved and the whole figure assembled.

249.
The figure in place on the stem. A temporary bowsprit has been fitted to help with the positioning.

250.
Milliput, rolled very thin, was used to apply his cape. It's now set and being further finished with a fine burr.

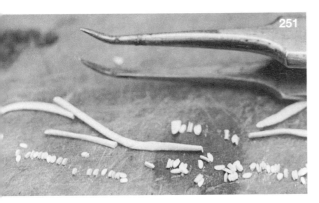

251.
For the decoration between the cheeks, two scrolls carrying the Prince of Wales's motto were required plus another two coats of arms. These were all made and painted at this stage together with the stern coats of arms. A number of leaves were also needed for the decorative 'vines'. I made these, as can be seen here, by rolling out some Milliput, then, just before it set, flattening the rolls slightly and slicing off separate leaves.

252.
The yellow mouldings on the cheeks have been cut from thin paper before painting and are here being glued in place. This gives a good clean finish which is almost impossible to achieve by hand painting.

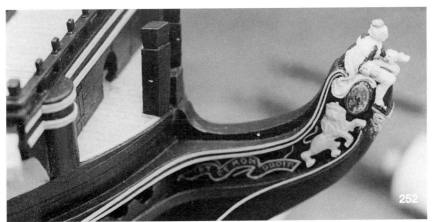

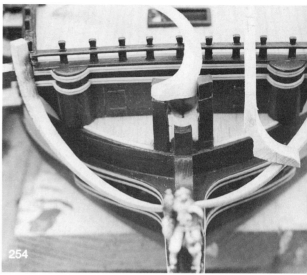

253.
The figurehead completed. Milliput, wire and paper have been used to construct crown, orb and sceptre.

254.
Now to shaping and fitting the rails. As is so often the best practce, they are cut oversize before shaping. Repeatedly, the rails are temporarily fitted, checked by measurement and eye, and then removed for reworking.

The middle rails, seen here resting on top of the model, were made in two pieces. The cathead support was first cut roughly to shape from a larger block of holly before being glued to the rail with a long scarph. This join is just visible. They are then further shaped with a small drum sander.

255.
Trying to heat-bend timber in the manner I have demonstrated in Nos 185-186 becomes more difficult as the thickness of the timber increases. I have overcome this difficulty with the thicker sections of rail by cutting a series of slots along the convex side with a razor saw, bending the timber and then running superglue into the slots to fill them.

256.
The middle and lower rails are installed. Not only do the fore and aft curves need to be considered, but a convex curve from the top rail to the upper cheek also has to be created otherwise it will be impossible to fit the head timbers correctly.

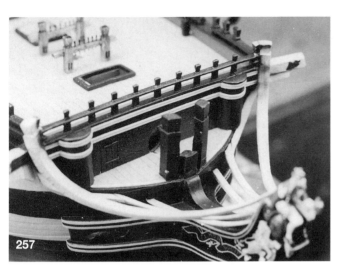

257.
The view from above. Note that the middle rail has again been cut and rejoined, allowing the upper end to follow round the bow of the ship, before changing direction and curving upwards towards the figurehead.

258.
The head timbers being fitted. I choose to fit each one in three stages. First, I glued a thin strip of wood into place on the outside of the rails and then cut and fitted individual filling pieces between the rails from above.

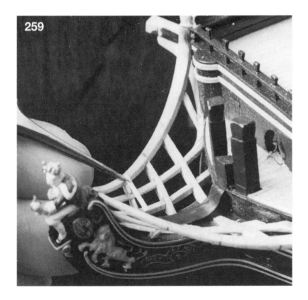

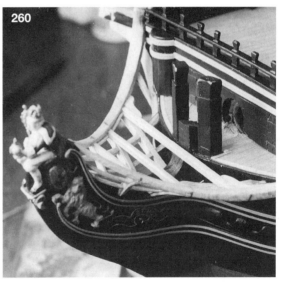

259.
Finally, a thin strip of timber is laid over the top of both filling pieces and rails. The whole assembly is then cleaned up with very fine needle files.

260.
Before fitting the head beams they were rebated on either side to form ledges which will accommodate the gratings. Ledges have also been fitted around the knees and along the inside edge of the top rail.

261.

Conduits for the seats of ease have been made from boxwood. They were drilled along their length before the holes were squared with a small diamond burr and file. This feature can be clearly seen, from below, in photograph 273. The gratings have been cut from boxwood strip and individually fitted.

262.
The remaining seats of ease are in place and false rails cut and ready for fitting.

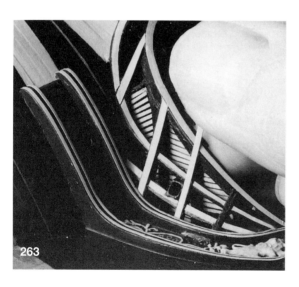

263.
The yellow bands being applied to the rails and head timbers, again using pre-painted paper. Next, blue paper will be cut, into even narrower strips, and laid over the yellow bands on the head timbers. This, apart from the painting, completes the work on the head for the present.

264.
Another small job that needs doing is the modelling of the motif on the ends of the catheads. This is seen being worked in Milliput.

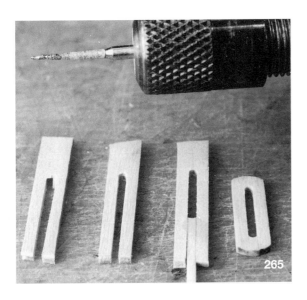

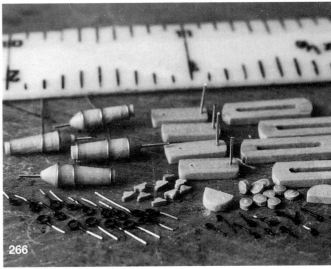

Carronades, Ropes and Boats

265.
It is now time to build the carronades, but much of the work is the same as outlined for the cannons. Here the slides are being made.

From the left: A strip of boxwood slotted on the Preac saw; the end of the slot rounded with a diamond burr, a strip glued into the slot; and, finally, the slide cut off and rounded.

266.
The various parts ready for assembly. Note the wires inserted in the base of the barrels which will eventually pass down through the holes in the carriages, through the slots in the slides and then be glued into pre-drilled holes in the deck. I use a similar method for the long guns, but with these the wire or dowel is fitted after the gun is glued in place and the hole is drilled down through the vent of the barrel, stool bed, bolster, axel-tree and deck. The wire or dowel is then dipped in glue before pushing it home. After cutting off, filing flush and painting, this fixing is quite invisible.

267.
A carronade in place. I always fit the breaching ropes, including their ring bolts, before installing the gun. When it is finally in place the eyebolts can be glued into the pre-drilled holes in the bulwarks.

268.
Now to prepare some of the coils of rope that will be required around the model. I first prepare long 'springs' of wire of various diameters and thicknesses using drill shanks and a Minicraft drill.

269.
These are then cut into short lengths, flattened and arranged in a life-like semblance of rope coils.

270.
To prepare coils to hang over belaying pins I shape them as shown around a pin driven into the edge of a block of boxwood.

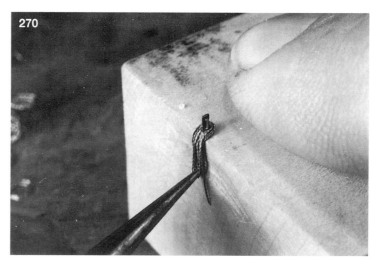

271.
Narrow strips of double-sided tape are run along the edges of some scrap card. Then the coils are temporarily attached to these while being painted. I prefer to use the airbrush for this job as it gives a far superior and more professional finish to that which can be achieved by hand painting.

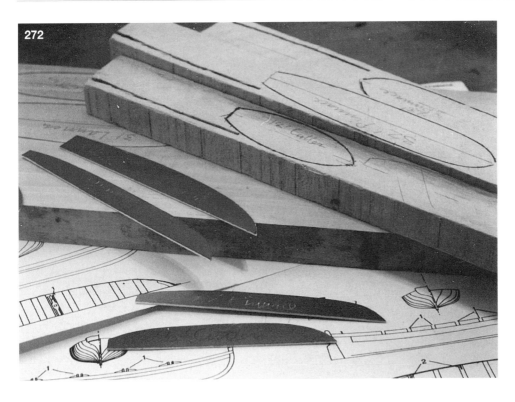

272.
Now to move on to the ship's boats. These are a modelling project in their own right so I packed the hull of *Majestic* safely away for a while and treated them as such.

I have, in the past, used various methods for the construction of ship's boats. I have built them over a male former from gummed paper; hollowed them from the solid; built them in two halves with keel, stem and the sternpost sandwiched between; and more usually moulded the hull from A.B.S. plastic. The latter is the method I am using for *Majestic*'s

boats. Six boats are required: a 31ft launch, a 32ft and 28ft pinnace, two 25ft and one 18ft cutters. The cutters were clinker-built whilst the others were carvel.

Before making a start on the actual construction of the boats I prepare templates for each: a half plan, a profile and a midship section.

The first stage of construction is to prepare some suitable fine-grained hardwood. I have used lemonwood and have marked out the hull shape in plan. The hulls are then carefully cut out.

273.
The profile has now been marked on both sides of the boat. The underbody will be cut to shape, but not the sheer. The wedge of wood above the sheerline and the sheerline itself needs to be retained throughout the shaping.

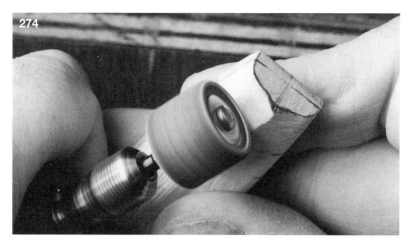

274.
I find that this work is best done with the small rotary sanding attachments in the Minicraft drill. The drum sander is useful when working under the counter . . .

275.
. . . and the disk for most of the other work.

276.
The hull is, of course, finished by hand.

277.
Two screws have been fitted to each hull. These will form handles for use when moulding.

The card trays have been made as a retainer for the epoxy car body filler which is used to make the female moulds.

278.
The trays have been filled with body filler and, after being thoroughly waxed, the wooden hulls are plunged into the filler and held firmly in place until it begins to set. Very soon after this happens they are pulled and prized free.

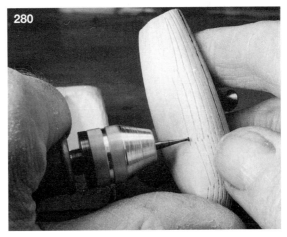

279.
The female moulds, after a little cleaning up, are now finished. The wooden plugs, however, have yet to be reduced in size. To aid me with this job I took an old dental burr similar to the one on the left and ground it down until it resembled the one on the right. When passed across wood this now cuts a narrow groove barely a 50th of an inch deep.

280.
The tool in use. The hulls are scored all over to a constant depth. The hull is then sanded down until all the groves disappear leaving a male mould that is an easy fit within the female.

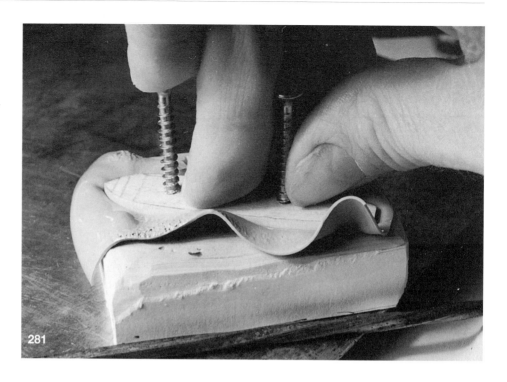

281.

With the moulds now completed we can now cast the hulls. Should you be doing this for the first time and be having little success – persevere. The key to a perfect result is softening the A.B.S. plastic just the right amount.

First, both parts of the mould are liberally rubbed over with candle wax and the female placed on a baking tray. A small sheet of A.B.S. plastic is them laid over the mould and it is placed under a grill. Watch carefully; if the edges of the plastic start to curl upwards, remove and turn the plastic sheet over before proceeding. This is because on heating the plastic tends to curve in one direction only regardless of the side from which the heat is applied. The secret is to get the sheet as soft as possible, but stop just *before* it starts to bubble. These bubbles permanently pock-mark the plastic on cooling. If it happens only around the edges, as in this photograph, there should not be a problem. When the plastic is ready remove it from the grill, place on a firm surface and immediately plunge the male mould into the softened sheet. If any of the results are at all suspect, make another. The whole process takes only seconds.

282.
Castings as removed. A sharp knife should be used to trim away the excess.

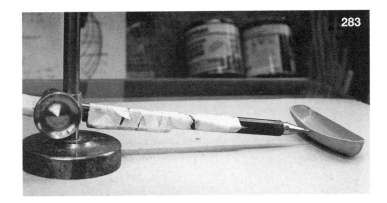

283.
Here I am marking the height at bow, stern and midship on both sides before drawing in the sheer and finally trimming to size.

284.
The completed castings. These need washing in hot soapy water and then cleaning thoroughly with a small stiff brush and some scouring powder. This will remove all trace of wax. Finally, they are rubbed down inside and out with some fine 'wet and dry'.

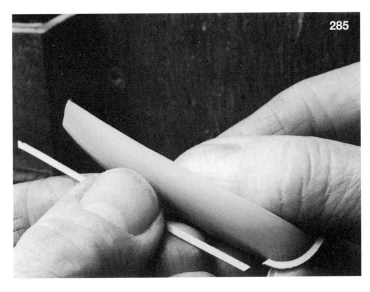

285.
The keel and stem being fitted. These are made from boxwood. A triangular wedge is made to fit between keel and counter.

286.
The stemson being fitted. A small wedge of wood has been fitted to the stempost. When the glue is dry this will all be trimmed to shape and then sanded.

287.
An epoxy filler has been used to give a smooth transition from keel to hull.

288.
The positions of the thwarts are next marked on the interior of the hulls and the rowlocks cut out. Then timber for gunwales, wash strakes and frames is prepared. This was all cut to size on the Preac saw and glued in place with Super-glue.

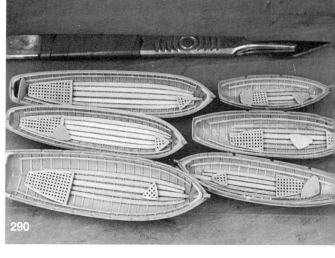

290.
The sternsheet transoms have been cut to size. One can be seen propped in place in the longer pinnace. The gratings have also been cut to size and have had boxwood framing fitted around them. This is quite a tricky and surprisingly exacting job. Thin ply or card templates should be made first.

289.
Knees, for both bow and stern, are cut to fit and glued in place in the form of a solid triangle. I then trim them to shape, first with a fine carbide cutter, and then finish them with a diamond burr.

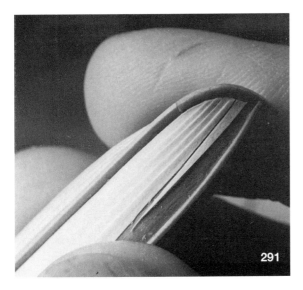

291.
I used some very thin card to suggest the clinker plank-ing on the cutters. After fitting each plank it was trimmed at the bow as can be seen in the photograph. The triangle of waste card was then removed. When fit-ting the next plank it will butt against this one at the bow, only overlapping it as it proceeds aft.

292.
The planking completed.

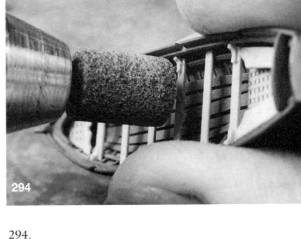

293.
One problem occured with the 32ft pinnace. This was fitted with a central 'bench'. This would have been joggled into the thwarts so as to finish flush with them but this is not really feasible at this scale. I overcame it by fitting a narrower 'false bench' beneath the thwarts and then fitting the bench itself, in sections, over the top and between the thwarts.

294.
The thwart knees were treated in the same man-ner as those at bow and stern. They were fitted as simple triangles before being initially shaped with this stone . . .

295.
. . . and then finished with a diamond burr.

296.
The sternsheets of the pinnaces were panelled and decorated with pre-painted paper in the same manner as the headwork's. The same treatment will be given to the washboards when they have been fitted.

297.
A rudder, with pintles and straps, being made. The end of the straps, filled with fine wood inserts, have yet to be drilled to accept the pintles.

298.
Each of the rowlocks for the pinnaces was made from four separate sections. Once again only being shaped after installation.

299.
I made the oars from boxwood. A strip was prepared and marked as shown, then the Preac saw was set to the required depth of cut and the piece of wood repeatedly run across the blade. Obviously, for this to work the strip of wood has to be left at its original thickness at either end.

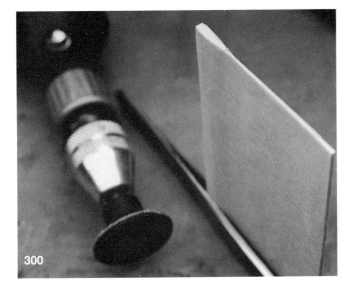

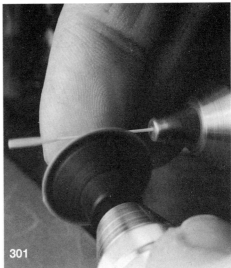

300.
The wood was then sanded down either side. Individual oars can then be sliced from this shaped piece of wood on the preac saw.

301.
Each oar was then mounted in a drill chuck and 'turned' with a rotary sander. It was then reversed and the remainder of the shaft finished, with a handle incorporated in the end. Finally, the blade was finished by hand with a file and sandpaper.

302.
A finished oar.

303.
Boats, oars and spare spars completed and ready for installation on the skid beams.

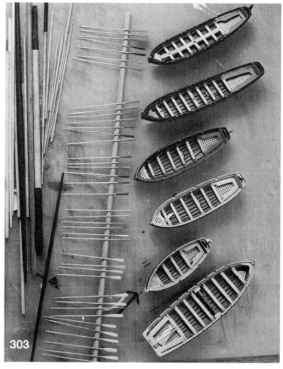

Hammock Netting and Other Details

304.
A prominent feature of late eighteenth-century men-of-war were the hammock nettings. All of these on my model will be shown with canvas covers. Blanks of balsa wood were used to represent them. They were fitted to the hull using spikes made from brass wire. These were glued into holes drilled in the hull. After cutting the balsa wood to size, I glued thin sections of plastic rod either side to suggest the cranes.

305.
The balsa was then scalloped and generally distressed using a rounded cutter. All the 'nettings' are then covered with black tissue paper to represent canvas. This was glued into place with P. V. A. adhesive. This allows a few creases and folds to be developed, giving a softer, more realistic representation. When dry they are finally impaled and glued in position on their spikes.

306.
The galley funnel was turned from a boxwood dowel. This was then cut and reassembled at 90 degrees. It was hollowed out, as far as possible, with this small round burr and a brass wire rim made and fitted.

307.
The fire buckets across the front of the poop were made as follows. A strip of Boxwood dowel was chucked and turned, as shown, using the rotary drum sander. It was then hollowed out with a diamond burr. The bucket was finished with a fine file and sandpaper before being parted off with a sharp knife. The leather strap handles were made from paper and the brackets to hang them on from brass wire. The brackets were glued on top of the poop rail and 'sandwiched' between it and the hammock nettings.

308.
The completed head. Some of the features worth noting are the netting either side of the beakhead (for which I used curtain netting painted black), the boomkins and the hearts for the mainstay and main preventer stay. I had not made provision for this last feature when constructing the head so that I now had to reach between head timbers and rails to drill a hole in the gammoning knee. This proved to be quite a problem. It was eventually accomplished by grinding down the shank of a drill all but about ⅟₁₆in at the tip. This was inserted between the timbers before switching on the drill, leaving the thin and harmless shank to revolve between the vulnerable timbers. A problem overcome! But better forward planning would have made the job easier.

There are some little figures in this photograph. I have not described them in the text, as this is not a realm I have ventured into before and neither is it one I can claim any expertise in. These were cast for me. My only involvement was to customise many of them for the various tasks they are undertaking and, of course, to paint them. Their real value is to give scale to the model.

309.

The completed hull aft. Several of the smaller fittings made earlier and set aside can here be seen fitted.

The fire buckets are all installed on their hooks. Coils of rope have been strategically glued to the decks and the hanks glued over the pins in the pinrails. Shot racks have been fitted around the hatches on the forecastle, quarterdeck and poop, and the hammock nettings glued in place.

It is almost certain that *Majestic* had not, at this time, been fitted with a built-up poop, but had the open rail, shown on the plans and depicted on the model. It is a matter of conjecture as to whether, at any one time, it would have been left open or covered with either netting or canvas. I think that while under sail, but not actually anticipating action, the rail would have been left open. This would certainly have enhanced her sailing performance under most conditions. During action, however, the rails would most likely be built up with 'junk' (old rope). This would have been enclosed and held in place either with netting, canvas or even, possibly, temporary panels or planks, in order to give some protection to the gun crews. I have depicted the ship at anchor and chose to fit plain canvas dodgers to these rails.

310.
This midship view also clearly shows the hammock nettings with their
canvas covers in place. Note also the ropes on and around the main
mast bitts and the hand ropes down to the upper gundeck and those
fitted to the side ladders. The most noticeable addition, however, has
been the fitting of the boats; I have installed three on the skid beams.
The small pinnace and two of the cutters will be shown afloat; their
exact positions not being determined until the sea is carved.

The lashing down of the boats to their skid beams was greatly facil-
itated by the method of their installation. If you remember, the beams
have been drilled, and are seated on the upturned ends of the piano
wire support brackets. These were first put in place on the model and
then the chocks for the boats were prepared and glued to the boats
(checking very carefully their position) and then to the skid beams.
Spare spars, timber, bundles of oars etc. were also glued to the beams
with tiny spots of super-glue.

The whole structure of beams, boats and spars was lifted free of the
brackets before lashing each item in place to the beams. This process
made an otherwise tricky and frustrating job very straightforward.

I do not like to permanently fit the beam ends until the last possible minute. It provides valuable access to the gundeck for any further
work that may need doing, the retrieval of dropped items and, last
but not least, 'dusting and cleaning'.

310

Carving the Sea

The next job to be tackled is the carving of the sea. I usually use lime or basswood for this. Whatever wood is used it needs to be fine grained and reasonably easy to carve.

For this model I used basswood, as I already had two well-seasoned planks set aside for this purpose. Owing to the size of the sea, 33in by 16in, it was necessary to join the two planks edge to edge. These edges were planed square and then grooved on the circular saw. A tongue (approximately 1in by ¼in) was then prepared to fit and bridge the two grooves. The whole assembly was then glued and clamped together and set aside to dry. This was actually done a couple of months earlier to give the timber plenty of time to settle. Now, returning to the work, the timber is marked out and cut to the correct dimensions, the edges and the underside planed square and flat.

311.
Next, battens are fitted to the underside, one at either end and one in the middle, to ensure that the plank remains flat. To allow for any expansion or contraction of the 16in-wide sea, care must be taken in their fixing. Examination of this photograph should help to make this clear. Two screws only on each batten are inserted through pre-drilled holes. These are placed about 1in either side of the join in the basswood plank. The remaining screws are fitted through routed slots. This form of fixing should allow for any lateral expansion and contraction of the timber to take place without warping.

312.
The board right-side up. A little time has to be spent deciding on the exact position of the hull and the ship's boats. When this is finally settled on, two holes are drilled in the board for the fixing rods in the base of the model, which can then be placed in position on the board and the base of the model marked on it. A template is then prepared from the lines plan to the outline of the hull about ⅛in above the water-line. This is used to make a second outline on the board. The first depicts the base of the model and the second a longitudinal section about ⅜in above it. I then set the router to this depth and removed a recess for the model, only removing wood inside the line representing the base of the model.

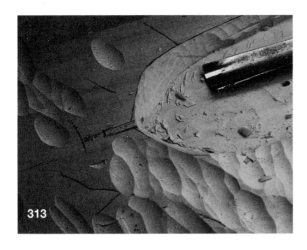

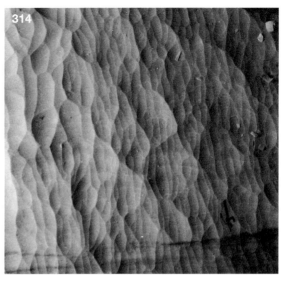

313.
A gouge is now used to remove the wood between the upper outside line and the base of the recess. Continual reference to the model itself will help in creating the correct contour. Also to be seen in this photograph are my guideline markings for the wave crests. The first stage of carving the sea is in progress.

314.
An area of the sea during the carving process. On the left can be seen the first rough cut while, on the right, smaller wavelets have been introduced.

315.
When satisfied with the carving, the hull is set in the sea. To ensure a perfect fit I usually employ the following method. A strip of cling-film is fixed around the hull below the waterline. This is held in place with a few tabs of double-sided tape. This needs to be reduced to a ' low tack' surface where it will adhere to the hull, so not to damage paintwork or coppering. This is easily achieved by repeatedly pressing the tape onto the palm of the hand. Some long coils of Milliput are then rolled out and pressed in place around the inside top edge of the recess. A coil is also laid either side of each of the holes for the fixing rods; then the hull is carefully repositioned and nuts fitted to the screwed rods beneath the sea. These are then tightened until the model settles at the right depth. A sharpened wooden tool is then used to trim away excess Milliput.

316.
When the Milliput is dry the hull can be removed from the sea and the cling film dispensed with.

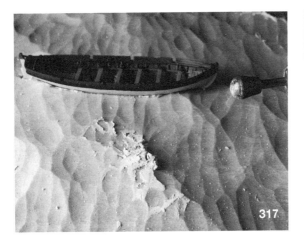

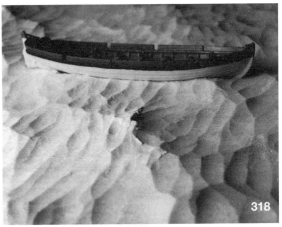

317.
The same process is now applied to the ship's boats and any breaking crests are also built up with Milliput. When dry the diamond burr, seen here just in front of the bow of the boat, is used to blend the crests into the waves.

318.
The completed crests.

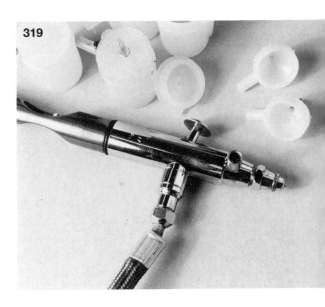

319.
Now all that remains is to paint the sea. I prefer to use enamel paints for this job. I'm afraid there is no recipe I can give for the actual application of the paint but I usually proceed as follows. First, the whole sea is given several coats of grey household undercoat, gently rubbed down between coats with fine wire wool. The sea is then painted quite freely with a coat of the overall colour I have chosen to use. When dry a second coat is applied but this time using two or three slightly different shades of the original colour. These can be blended together or applied in more delineated areas to represent cloud shadow on the water. Any white water around the hull and the wave crests is then added, blending in with brush, finger or dry brush. I then like to airbrush carefully across the crests of the waves with some very dilute paint, usually a little of the original colour mixed with some white. This needs to be done delicately, understatement being the order of the day. It need not be evenly applied over the whole sea but quite patchily. I think it gives the feeling of gusts of wind moving over the water, stippling the surface and reflecting light, and it certainly adds a little more life to the subject. Turning a block of wood into a living sea is an impossible task. We just do the best we can.

This might be a good place to say more about airbrushing. It is a technique I have used for years for certain limited applications. Until recently the more limit-

ed the better! My old airbrush was just not suitable for the model-makers' needs – whatever the manufacturers claimed. The enamels and acrylics I used clogged it so regularly that I spent more time dismantling and cleaning than spraying. Now I have a new airbrush and compressor. It is a Paasche custom MV #2. These are customised and supplied by the Airbrush and Spray Centre whose address can be found in the section on tools and materials at the back of the book. It will cover large areas with ease or draw a pencil-thin line. Its secret lies in its cutaway nozzle. This exposes the end of the needle and if any paint builds up on the tip it can be just wiped away between finger and thumb.

Masts, Spars, Yards and Rigging

320.
Throughout the final section of this work it will become apparent that the photographs and text are much less sequential than previously. This allows techniques to be described without too much repetition taking over; the making of a spar or block only needs to be described once. There are excellent books available detailing all the information you are likely to need when it comes to masting and rigging as outlined in the notes accompanying the masting and rigging plan on pages 112-113. You can make your own plan.

A friend obtained some lemon wood for me and I used this for the masts and spars. Previously, I have always used boxwood. Both work well.

321.
The lower masts were constructed as follows. A square piece of timber was mounted in the lathe between chuck and tailstock and the round section turned to the correct diameters. When I say turned, this invariably involves using a sanding disk in a Minicraft drill for rough shaping and then applying aluminium oxide paper of various grades, glued to wooden formers; for finishing. From the hounds upwards the mast was left square.

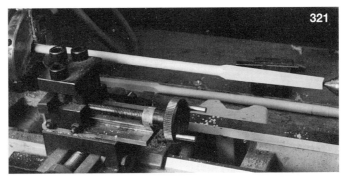

322.
At this stage I fitted the rubbing paunch and filling pieces. These were made as one unit. I had previously shaped some thin sheets of basswood by boiling them, binding them round various metal or plastic formers, and leaving them to dry in the airing cupboard overnight. A number of these can be seen in the centre of the picture. At the front a rubbing paunch has been cut and fitted to the mast. Note the flattened side ready to accept the cheeks.

323.
Then the cheeks and bibs were fitted, roughly shaped as can be seen in the photograph. The masthead was then reduced to the correct dimensions. All these fittings are still over-large as usual. I prefer reducing them to the exact dimensions after fitting.

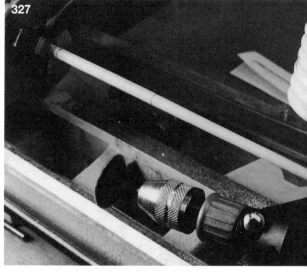

324.
Turning the topmasts is slightly more complex as there are square and octagonal sections at either end. Again, accurately finish the round section first.

325.
Then the remaining sections of the mast can be planed, trimmed and filed to the correct shape and section. These three sections show various stages of the work.

327.
The octagonal spar in the lathe with one end in the process of being turned.

326.
The first job to do when shaping spars is to produce octagonal stock of the correct dimensions. I found that, with care, most of this work could be achieved on the circular saw. Here a billet is being prepared for one of the lower yards.

327.
The octagonal spar in the lathe with one end in the process of being turned.

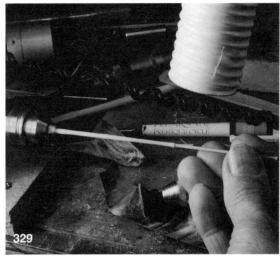

328
Once shaped, the spars are then detailed. Iron bands, made from black paper, have been fitted and the various cleats are being added. I prefer to shape these *in situ* on the spars.

329.
Topgallant, pole-masts, studding sail booms etc are again turned using the sanding disks. Instead of support from a tailstock, however, they can be lightly supported between the fingers while they are shaped.

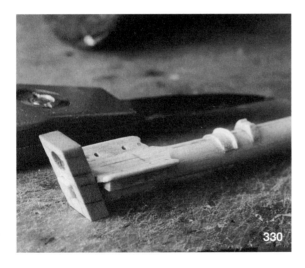

330.
The bowsprit is shaped in the same way as were the lower masts. Here the boxwood cap is in place. The bees were cut and fitted at the correct angle before fitting the blocks beneath them. Then the blocks were doweled to the bowsprit and the bees to the blocks. Also fitted are the saddles for the jibboom while the spritsail sling has also been fitted.

331.
Fairlead saddle and gammon cleats. Note the final finishing of all these items takes place after fitting.

332.
The same technique of shaping after assembly is here being applied to the boom and gaff jaws.

333.
The rope wooldings around the lower masts and bowsprit are quite straightforward to apply. They are started by first tucking the end under the following turns and are completed by means of the loop of thread shown. This should lie under the last two turns. The end of the woolding is passed through the loop and pulled back under the last two turns before trimming off.

334.
The wooldings after application are given a coat of matt paint. This is smeared round by finger, bedding down any loose fibres. Finally, wooden batons made from pre-painted paper can be fitted.

335.
One final aspect of spar construction that can be problematical is the fitting of studding sail booms and irons. I have made these in many ways in the past but have found the following method as easy, strong and trouble free as any. From the top of the picture to the bottom: the end of the spar is drilled and an L-shaped wire bracket fitted. The boom is then drilled and fitted to the bracket which is then glued in place and the end cut off; another hole is drilled and a pin fitted by way of the inboard iron and, finally, irons of black paper are glued around the boom.

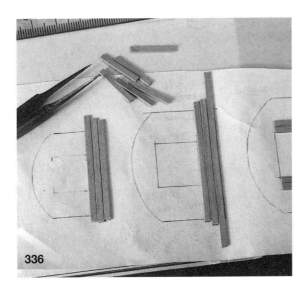

336.

337.

336.

Tops are rather more complicated structures than they initially appear, particularly when painted black. This is how I chose to build mine. The tops were first of all marked out on writing paper and the planked areas built up by gluing in place with super-glue. When all the planks have been laid I turned the paper over and applied another coat of super-glue to the undersides, wiping away any excess. Fast!

337.

The original markings on the paper are clearly visible through the glue-saturated paper and are used to trim the tops to shape. The next job, cutting the curved rim to fit over the front of the top, is a little tricky. I found the best way to overcome this was to make it over thick and then thickness it on the circular saw before fitting. A 'thick' rim can be seen on the left of the picture. Next, battens are prepared (foreground), and a rebate cut at one end and fitted to overlap the rim (centre). Instead of then fitting filling pieces between these – quite impractical – I trimmed them just short of the edge of the rim and glued a thin batten around the top outside edge of the top. Now using some fine sanding boards I tapered the battens towards the centre of the top. This makes a real difference to the appearance at this scale.

338.

339.

338.

The tops, crosstrees and trestletrees. The construction is straightforward and the photograph should be self explanatory. The curves in the topmast crosstrees were induced using the soldering iron technique as demonstrated in Nos 185-186.

339.

A completed top in place at the masthead with rail, bolster and swivel gun chock added. Square holes, such as those required for the swivel guns, can be drilled round and then punched square with a home-made tapered punch.

Before starting on the rigging I settled down to make all the various blocks, deadeyes and hearts that would be required. I decided early on that I would make these from boxwood, using methods similar to those usually employed when building larger models. In practice this proved to be a quite straightforward, if somewhat time-consuming, task. The first job is to produce stock of the right dimensions for the various blocks and then to groove them appropriately.

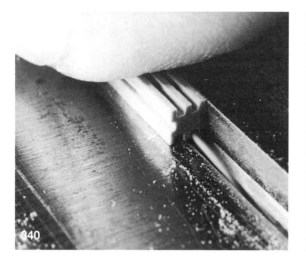

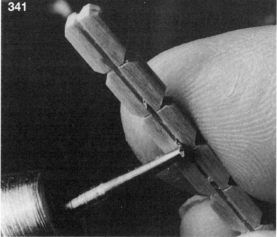

340.
Here timber is being grooved for a double block. Similar stock is prepared for singles, trebles, hearts etc.

341.
After cutting the grooves, the length of each block was marked in and a V cut at each intersection with a sharp knife. This star-shaped cutter was then used to deepen the groove at either end of the strop groove.

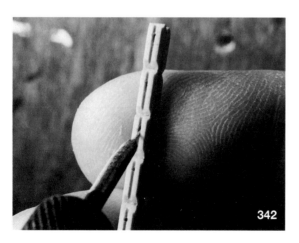

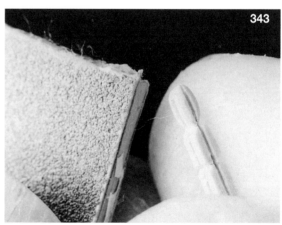

342.
The blocks are next drilled for the ropes and, as shown here, the edges of the hole rounded off.

343
Finally, the blocks are shaped with a sanding board before parting off. For these demonstration pictures I have obviously chosen the very largest blocks for clarity. The process, however, is identical with the smaller ones.

344.
A selection of blocks under construction.

346.
The masts were assembled and painted, stained and varnished. They were then drilled where the spars were to be fitted, as were the spars. Brass pegs were then glued into the holes in the spars so that they could be fitted, removed and relocated easily, the pegs only being glued into the masts on final assembly. All the details that could be added at this stage were then fitted to the masts.

The mast coats, turned and drilled on the lathe are first glued in place with the masts in position in the hull. Then, as this photograph shows, strips of boxwood are prepared from which to cut the ribs for the upper yard parrels. These were shaped across the grain and the individual ribs sliced from them on the circular saw. The trucks are tiny balls of Milliput. Fitting them was simplicity itself. First, a rib was glued in place, then a pair of trucks, another rib, and so on. Referral to the final rigging photographs should make this clear. Main topsail yard and fore topgallant yard parrels can be seen completed in Nos 372-375. All the items listed on page 106 should then be fitted to the masts. I always seem to manage to omit at least one of them, always in the most inaccessible position imaginable, which then has to be installed at a later date through a spiders web of rigging.

345.
Some of the completed blocks. They will now need to be stained or painted and then stropped. The best way to stain these tiny items is to put them in a small jar (one size at a time) with a little stain and stir with a brush. They can then be tipped out onto absorbent paper, moved around a little to remove any excess stain, and left to dry.

347.
Before proceeding with the fittings on the masts the furled driver needs to be shaped and installed. For sails I use tissue paper with the individual cloths drawn in with a 7H pencil. The paper is then sprayed with successive coats of a diluted matt acrylic medium with tiny additions of acrylic paint. I allow this to build up on the tissue until achieving the patina and colour I require. During spraying the paper is mounted on a wooden frame to allow both sides to be treated. The end result is strong enough to allow quite a lot of pulling and shaping even when wet. Tissue paper is thin

enough, even for a miniature model, to allow for tabling, reef bands etc. to be cut and glued to the sail without it appearing over heavy. The photograph shows a template, roughly the size and shape of the piece of tissue required to form the furled driver sail. The sail itself is in the process of being shaped. It is being slowly teased into shape while damp, and short lengths of wire are being used to draw the sail to the gaff and mast where the brails will later be fitted. The clew of the sail is made separately and will be glued into a fold in the sail later.

DETAILS TO BE FITTED TO THE MASTS

BOWSPRIT ASSEMBLY
Collars and hearts for forestay and preventer stay.
Collars and deadeyes for bobstays and shrouds.
Jibboom heel lashing.
Blocks and thimbles for all the foremast bowlines.
Jibboom footropes.
Jib stay outhauler and traveller.
Block for fore topgallant stay.
Blocks for the spritsail lifts.

FOREMAST
Truss for fore yard.
    This item, like many others made from wire, will be fitted in several parts and at different stages of the rigging process. In this instance only the section of truss around the mast is fitted. As soon as the mast is finally glued in place in the hull it will be continued down to deck. The remaining section, of course, will be on the fore yard.
Parrels for upper yards.

Blocks for main topmast stay and preventer.
Block for main topgallant stay.
Blocks under the top for lower bunts, leeches and spritsail braces.
Long tackle blocks at the masthead for lower lifts.
Blocks for the topgallant lifts.
Double blocks for the topmast buntlines.
Blocks for main topsail and topgallant sail bowlines.

MAINMAST
Deadeye for mizzen stay.
Thimble for preventer.
Thimble for mizzen topmast stay.
Thimble for mizzen topgallant stay.
Truss for main course.
Parrels for upper yards.
Long tackle blocks for the lower lifts.
Blocks for mizzen topgallant bowlines.
Blocks for fore topmast staysail halliard.
Double blocks for topsail bunt lines.
Double blocks under the top for the main course bunt and leech lines.

MIZZEN MAST
Pendants for main topsail braces.
Blocks for crossjack lifts.
Blocks for topsail bunts.
Blocks for topgallant lifts.
Blocks for top mast and topgallant braces.
Parrels for the gaff and boom (small balls of Milliput).
Blocks for the brails.
Gaff peak halliard.
Gaff throat halliard.
Boom topping lift.
Boom horses.
Driver sheet.

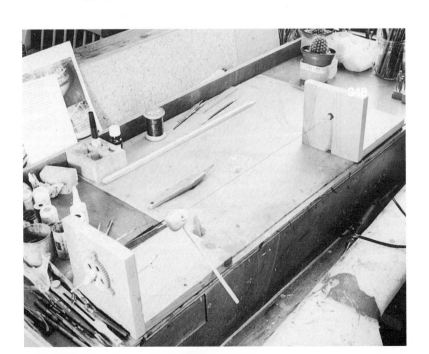

Rigging

348.
As I mentioned in the introduction, I intended experimenting with thread for the standing rigging and wire for running rigging, thus getting the best of both worlds. I

needed, therefore, to assemble rigging material of the correct diameters. The running rigging would not be a problem as I had all the sizes of tinned copper wire needed for its preparation.

I know some modelmakers prefer nickel chrome and alloy wires for this job. I have tried them and I am sure they have their uses. I personally don't like them as a medium for representing rope. They may last well into the third millennium and beyond but seem to me too hard and springy for this job. I prefer the softer, more responsive and compliant qualities of copper. I find it more controllable, whether trying to ensure that shroud and stays are straight, or at best only show a slight downward curve or when trying to develop the more extreme curves sometimes required for running rigging.

My stock of thread, however, was more limited. Over thirty years ago I had scoured obscure shops in the east end of London searching for linen thread of a suitable quality for rigging the ¼in and ⅛in to the foot models I was building at that time. I still have a lot of this and I really do not know where it could be obtained nowadays. Although these threads, and multiples of them, served to produce the heavier ropes, I obviously needed something finer and eventually settled on silk and synthetic fly tying threads for the finer ropes. The photograph shows my very primitive rope walk which cost little in either time or money to make. I used plastic gear wheels and collars mounted on some brass rod for the winding end. The brass hooks were formed by grinding the rod flat and bending with pliers. The wheels and collars were initially glued in place with a spot of super-glue and I then drilled through the hub of the wheels as well as the brass rod before pinning right through with a length of piano wire. So far it has stood the test of time. The looper is a small hook in the end of a strip of dowel. This was glued into a ball race from a skate board wheel and this, in turn, was mounted in the tail end of the walk. When in use the winder is screwed or clamped in place and the tail end allowed to slide towards it along the bench. Various weights can be added to the wooden platform depending on the thickness of the rope that is being made. The top is carved from balsa wood, the grooves being smoothed and rubbed with candle wax before use.

This is scant information on a topic which, in its own right, is a whole subject but others have written at great length and expertise on the subject.

All the running rigging was prepared several months in advance and then, using various weights, left to stretch before use.

So now with the blocks made, some of them already stropped with wire rigging, and plenty of thread and wire rigging material also prepared, the process of rigging the model can begin.

349.
The detailed masts have been glued into the hull and lengths of rope for the shrouds are here fitted around the foremast head. They are secured by a small whipping. They are put on in pairs apart from the last one which is single, and not yet bedded down on the others.

350.
I constructed this very simple jig to enable all the upper deadeyes to be tied in at a uniform height above the lower ones. The strip of wood is fixed temporarily in place by drilling through several of the deadeyes on the channel and into the jig, then fitting short lengths of brass wire through both. Next, a horizontal line is marked on the jig to establish the height of the upper deadeyes above the channel. Each shroud in turn is drawn down over the centre of the lower deadeyes and marks made where they cross the horizontal line. Holes are drilled at these points.

To tie in a deadeye, a brass wire pin is inserted, as shown, through the upper hole in the upper deadeye being fitted and the relevant hole in the jig, so positioning it temporaryily while the shroud is drawn taught around it. It can then be grasped with another pair of tweezers, trapping the shroud in place, then be pulled free of the pin and a small whipping applied.

351

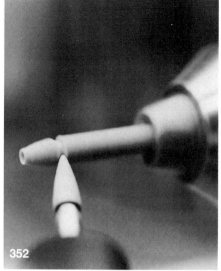

352

351.

The lanyards being reeved. They are only finally adjusted and tied off when they have all been fitted. This same process is repeated for all three masts and the bowsprit.

There is one other job to be done before moving on and that is the fitting of the rigging cleats to the shrouds inboard and just above the deadeyes. These are only required for the fore- and mizzen mast, the mainmast having pinrails. I had some that had been brass-etched but they could equally be cut from wood or made from wire. I slotted the shaft of each between the shroud and its up-turned end and glued them in place with super-glue.

352.

The lower fore-and-aft stays are quite straightforward to make and fit. A mouse will be required for most of them. One is here being drilled and turned using a diamond burr.

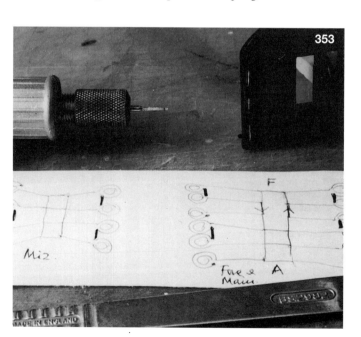

353

353.

The next job is the fitting of the deadeyes for the topmast shrouds. One length of rope will now form all the deadeye strops, futtock shrouds and catharpins. I prepared this little diagram to help me with the job. The circles are deadeyes, the lines running between them the rope lanyard and the two lines crossing them the futtock staves. The short, very dark lines represent the grooves cut underneath the tops, as can be seen underneath the top in the background. The following photograph and text should make this all clear.

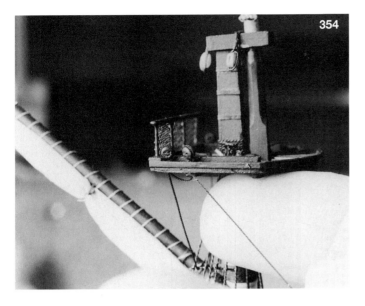

354.
In practice the thread is knotted and passed up through the aft hole at the other side of the top, taken around a deadeye, thus forming a strop and then down through the same hole to the futtock stave; so producing a futtock shroud. Now the rope leads athwartships to the opposing stave, as a catharpin. It is then brought up through the aft starboard hole, again around a deadeye and again down through the same hole, but this time after doing so leading forward under the rim before forming the strop for the next deadeye forward. This photograph shows the process at this stage. The loop under the top has yet to be drawn tight; when it is it will bed down flush in its groove. When I had finished fitting the deadeyes to a top and was satisfied with the result, the position where the ropes crossed the futtock staves was checked and a spot of super-glue applied both here and where the ropes passed through the tops.

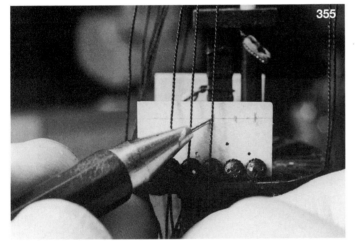

355.
A jig, as used for the lower shrouds, being prepared for the top mast.

356.
Topmast lanyards rigged but final tightening has not yet taken place.

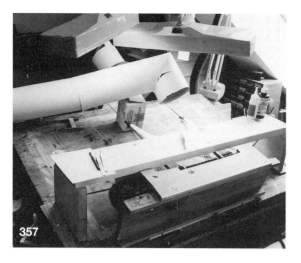

357.

I finally decided not to clove hitch the ratlines using fine thread but to attempt to glue fine wire directly to the shrouds. This was an attempt to develop a greater scale of realism and to allow the ratlines to hang more naturally between the shrouds. Before starting work on this I mounted an old drawing board on my work bench and screwed the base on which the model was mounted down to it, positioned on its side. A shelf was made on which I could rest my arms whilst doing this job. The shelf could easily be unscrewed from the drawing board and repositioned higher up the masts as the work progressed. The cardboard extension to my extractor fan was a blessing and took away some of the worst of the glue fumes.

358.

In practice, individual strips of prepared wire are laid across the shrouds and glued to one or two of them to hold them in place. I then work across the whole area with the little jig, demonstrated here. It simply holds the ratlines tight against a shroud allowing me to individually glue the ratlines to that shroud with super-glue which is applied with a very fine piece of wire held in a pin vice. The jig is in the form of two sides and a top. The other side is shorter so does not show in the photograph. The square is simply there to add weight.

The card guide shows the positions for each of the ratlines. A batten of wood has been laid across main and mizzen masts and a folded piece of card fitted between this and the guide. It acts as a gentle spring to hold the guide in place.

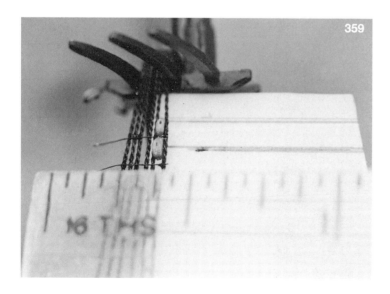

359.

This is a good time to fit the sister blocks (two singles) between the top-mast shrouds.

360.
Once the ratlines were completed, each loop was pressed down into a gentle curve with a small wooden tool I made for the job. The ends of the wires were, of course, neatly trimmed and I then used the airbrush to give another coat of black paint to the shrouds, lanyards, lower stays and tops, masking other areas when required.

I have also made some additions to my work base. The extension fore and aft protects the jib-boom and driver boom. They also serve as very convenient handles for manoeuvring the model. The pointed battens either side of the spritsail yard not only protect the spar but also provide a useful rest for the heel of the hand whilst working on the rigging on and around the head. The upright battens either side allow the model to be laid on its side. They are fixed to the base with only one screw each so that they can be easily angled down for better access to the rigging behind them. They also, in various positions, provide support whilst working. It looks rather crude and primitive, but serves its purpose.

361.
The next jobs to be tackled are the remaining fore-and-aft stays and the fitting of the gammoning to the bowsprit. The fitting of the loosely furled staysails also has to be done. Here a sail is being prepared. Tabling has been glued along the head and short lengths of painted rigging wire are being glued along its length. They will form the rope hanks around the stay.

362.
The sail has been dampened and is being fitted to its stay; the 'hanks' are being bent over the stay and arranged in place, one at a time, as is the zigzag folding down. When satisfied with the fitting to the stay I will work my way down the sail, fitting gaskets and settling the sail into its final position.

Other fore-and-aft stays are treated similarly, the only real deviation being the fitting the fore topmast staysail. This requires a section of netting to support the sail when furled, keeping it clear of the bowsprit. This was made from the same curtain netting used for the head and tops. It is shown clearly in No 373.

NOTES ON THE PREPARATION OF
A MASTING AND RIGGING PLAN

I have prepared this rigging plan for *Majestic* to give a general impression of the masts, yards and sails as I chose to rig them on the model. I must emphasise that it is not a complete plan that could be used alone to work from. A large and complex set is required to cover that ground. Neither is this the plan that I refer to in the text which is indeed a far more basic and messy affair but which is, incidentally, the type of plan I would recommend any modelmaker to compile before or whilst building a model of this period. Unfortunately most plans and models, including my own, contain mistakes. These may be major or minor, but, they are mistakes and when plans are worked from or the resulting model is used as reference material the 'Chinese Whisper' factor ensures and the final model is further distanced from the prototype. The best way to avoid contributing to this progression and, incidentally almost certainly producing a more accurate model, is to, firstly, build the hull using Admiralty Draughts for the ship and, secondly, to prepare your own rigging plans either using 'Lees' or 'Steel'.

Preparing a rigging plan really is not such a daunting task and can be produced as follows. First take a copy or tracing of the profile, cut it out and mount it at the bottom of a suitable piece of card, then using the ' proportions of masts, spars and rigging' at the back of 'Lees' or the Tables of Dimensions in 'Steel' (which can also be found in Marquardt's *18th Century Rigs and Rigging*), draw in the masts and yards. These do not need to be works of art, just ensure the diameters are correct at the slings and yard arms or even note these measurements beside the spar for future reference. Secondly, take several copies of the plan. One copy can then be used to draw in all the standing rigging and another two used for the running rigging. Using two copies ensures that there is less overcrowding and the final plans are easier to read. When drawing the rigging in, I like to note rope and block sizes plus any other information that limits the number of times that I have to go back and refer to the reference books, so that interruptions to the actual work on the rigging are limited.

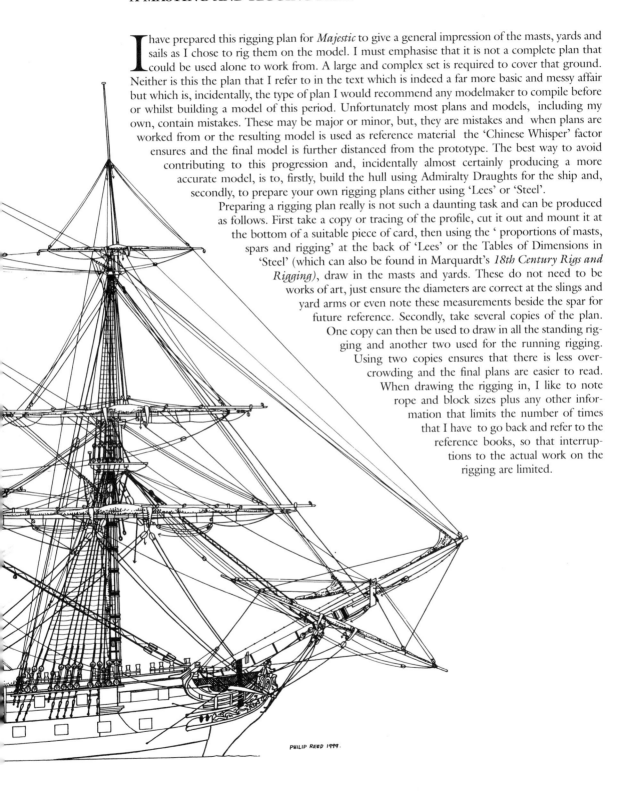

PHILIP REED 1999.

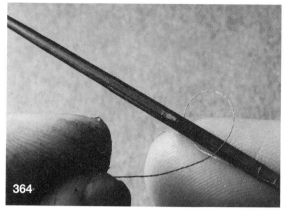

363.

The topmast stays, when brought down to the deck were, like many other items of rigging, fitted in several sections. Here halliards are being made up.

The hooks are formed on the single blocks from the tail ends of the strops. These were coated in super-glue and then shaped with a diamond burr. They will connect to eyebolts at the foot of the masts.

Before moving on to the spars all the rigging to the fore-and-aft sails and all the possible rigging to the square sails should be fitted and taken down to the deck. This latter will include lifts, bowlines, braces, buntlines etc. whose blocks are already in place on the masts. The boats on their spars can also be finally glued in place and the mainstay tackles fitted and brought down to the beams.

364.

As much detail as possible should be added to the spars before they go aloft. The first job is to fit the rowbands. This photograph should clearly demonstrate the method used. The thread linking each rowband can be positioned to lie beneath the sail.

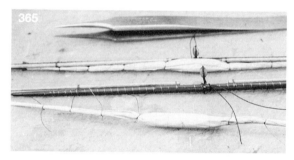

365.

Next, all the blocks stropped to the yards have to be fitted, or at least the sections of their strops that go around the yard.

I usually prefer, when working to this small scale, to simply fit the strops, leaving a small gap in the strop where the yard can be drilled. At a later stage the block can be fitted by simply inserting its strop into the hole and gluing it in place. However, particularly on the lower yards I preferred to strop and fit the larger blocks with thread. There is no hard and fast rule and the difference will not be apparent on the finished model. Here one topsail is being prepared and another has been fitted to its yard. Note the bulky centre. Topsails are large sails in relation to the size of their spars. This should be reflected when showing them furled.

366.

The clues of the sails are made separately. These are being prepared for the mainsail.

367

368

367
Clues ready to fit to the spritsail. They will be cut to length, tucked and glued under the top of the furled sail before being drawn forwards and down over it. One or two spots of glue should be sufficient to hold them in place.

368
Working on the lower yards. The yard in the foreground is mounted on a strip of balsa, the brass pin being pushed through the wood allowing the spar to lie flat. Positions for the footrope stirrups can be seen marked in on the balsa. When these are in place the spar will be reversed and the port stirrups fitted.

369
This photograph shows clearly all the details that should be accommodated on the spars before they are fitted to the mast, they are shown here approx actual size they are on the model.

370
Had I worked out how I intended to rig the jeers earlier I would have fitted this detail immediately after the lower shrouds and stays. At this late stage it is a little more difficult. Examination of this photograph reveals the end of the upper jeer block strop. Through it is threaded the lashing. Rather than try and feed this through the cleats, only the ends of these were glued to the mast while this was being done.

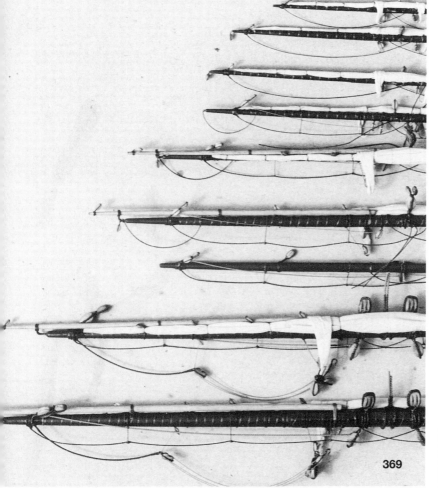

369

370

374

375

371.
Foremast.

372.
Mainmast.

373.
The bowsprit assembly.

374.
Mizzen mast.

375.
Fore topmast head and topgallant mast.

376.
Mizzen boom and gaff.

376

377.
The top of the cleat was then fitted, cleaned up with a small diamond burr and finally painted.

378.
Both jeer blocks have been rigged on the lower yards. Careful examination of the photograph will reveal that the strop around the upper block does not continue right across its top. At this point the block has been drilled to accept the end of the section of strop already lashed to the masthead. When the yard is correctly located on the mast these strops should fit neatly into place.

Now to complete the rigging of the model all that remains to do is to fit the yards to the masts and continue the running rigging from the blocks on the yards, either to other blocks on the masts, stays or shrouds or straight down to the deck. I prefer to start with the spritsail yard, completing all the rigging to the head before moving on to the courses, topsails and, finally, topgallants. I like to leave any very vulnerable ropes like the spritsail braces, course braces and gaff vangs till last.

Anchors and Stern Lanterns

379.
They should really have featured in the section on the hull, but because of their vulnerability I like to leave them until after the rigging is completed.

The anchors are made from boxwood. This is quite straightforward work, as can be seen here. The individual parts are in various stages of completion.

380.
After assembly, super-glue fillets can be run in between shaft and arms and final finishing is accomplished using burrs and stones. Then iron bands are fitted to the stocks and wire rings to the shanks. The ring on the completed and painted anchor has been bound over with thread.

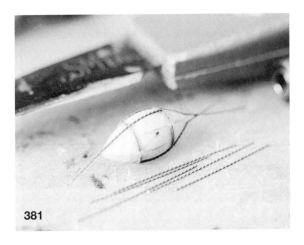

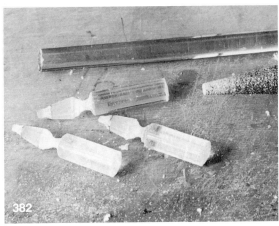

381.
An anchor buoy, turned from boxwood, being detailed with wire.

382.
I made the stern lanterns from Perspex rod, initially being roughly turned in the lathe before developing the octagonal shape with a file.

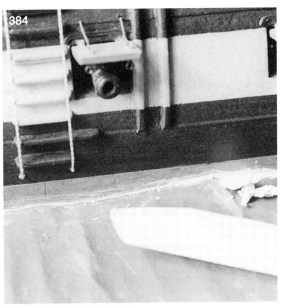

383.
The lanterns have been further refined and cleaned up using fine wet-and-dry paper. They are finally polished before being parted off and mounted on lengths of brass wire. All that now remains is to detail them using pre-painted strips of tissue.

384.
The completed model can now be set and bolted in its recess in the sea and the boats glued in place with Araldite. Any remaining gaps can then be filled. I prefer to use plasticine for this job. This photograph shows some being worked into the groove. Any slight residue left on the sea or ship is easily removed with a paint brush or cotton bud dipped in white spirit. A little of the original paint mix is then used to touch up blemishes and the whole sea is then given a final coat of gloss varnish.

The Flags

One final job is to make and fit the flags. The flags, like the sails, are made from tissue paper. After marking them out the tissue can be held in place on a flat surface with a few scraps of masking tape and then painted with acrylic paints.

The pennant presents a problem all of its own. Whereas the other flags can be persuaded to hang fairly naturally the pennant needs stiffening. I made it from a double layer of tissue glued together with super-glue and further stiffened by trapping two fine copper wires between the layers.

Prior to fitting, the flags are all generally distressed and crumpled several times before being teased to the required shape. I find that at this stage heat treating helps to maintain their shape. This is best done with a hair dryer. Unfortunately, they need holding to shape with the other hand! Once fitted the flags and all the rest of the rigging are given a light coat of matt varnish applied with the airbrush.

*   *   *

Epilogue

This all but concludes the work on the model except for finding and rectifying those minor omissions that almost inevitably occur during the rigging process. The whole project took me in excess of 2,000 hours spread over twenty-two months.

One feature that I have not mentioned is the protection of the model after it has been completed. I usually build my own glass display cases but on this occasion *Majestic* was heading for a purpose-built display case in the USA.

Photographing the Model

Firstly, I must make it quite clear that I am not an expert in this field. I take photographs nowadays to record my own work and to use them as a research tool.

Up until recently I used my 35-year-old Pentax Spotmatic with a standard 55mm lens and a set of extension tubes for close up work. For lighting I used either natural light or a couple of rickety photofloods. I got used to this set up and it worked perfectly well. Before starting this book, however, I replaced my camera with a more recent model. This is another 35mm. camera with manual as well as automatic functions. After two years I have yet to investigate the latter but am going to get around to it soon. Old habits die hard! The camera came with a 50mm lens but I have supplemented this, once again, with a set of extension tubes for the close-up work. I have used close-up lenses in the past but personally consider that extension tubes are superior both from the point of versatility and quality of image obtained. To enable me to cope better with the photographs taken for this book I also purchased a good 35-105mm zoom lens with a macro facility. This allowed me to take some of the close-up photographs using the macro facility, the workshop photographs at 35mm, to give the wide angle of view required, and the 105mm setting for the photographs of the completed ship at anchor. This eliminated the forced perspective inevitable with a shorter lens. I have also obtained, and had excellent results with, a polarising filter to cut out most of the unwanted reflections. Colour correcting filters were not used or required as most of the photographs were in black and white. The colour photographs were all taken using natural light. Those of the completed model were all taken indoors, close to a window. The model was placed on a sheet of board on top of a packing case to which several vertical battens had been screwed. These battens projected upwards several feet on two sides only. A large sheet of blue grey card was pinned to the battens to form a back drop and another large sheet of white card fixed to the remaining battens behind the model. This was used to reflect light on to the shaded side. This did not give perfect all round lighting such as can be obtained using a battery of lights but I actually prefer the more dramatic, natural side lighting.

I used Ilford XP2 for black and white photographs and Kodachrome for the colour. The 400 A.S.A. XP2 was used purely for convenience. It can be processed using C41 colour processing chemicals enabling the developing and printing to be carried out, usually within an hour, and at colour processing prices, in most high street photographic stores. This process produces a print with a slight sepia cast. It can, however, also be printed to give a black and white print. This is a little more expensive and usually takes longer. The Kodachrome was requested by my publisher, the positive film being better suited for reproduction. I usually, however, take colour negatives and have had good results with a variety of films as long as they have an A.S.A. of 200 or lower. My film of choice for many years was Ektar 25. However, I really don't think that, with modern film emulsions, the super slow films are much of an advantage unless they are required for considerable enlargement.

Mission accomplished. The finished model undergoing
a final inspection.
(Photography by Simon Burt, Apex Photo Agency Ltd)

MATERIALS AND TOOLS

Below is a list of suppliers of the tools and materials some of which have been mentioned in the text. I have not listed the suppliers of paints, adhesives, milliput, plastecene etc. as they are readily available in most arts and graphics shops or hardware stores and the type used is frequently dependent on personal choice.

In the UK

Douglas Electronic Industries Ltd. 55, Eastfield Road, Louth, Lincs LN11 7AL
Tel. (01507) 603643.
Can supply a suitable transformer (No. MT 69 WSP 25OVA) for use in the U.K. with the Preac Saw.

Maynard Ltd. Days Mill, Nailsworth. Nr. Stroud, Gloucestershire GL6 0BL
Tel. (01453) 833185.
Suppliers and repairers of Emco and Unimat lathes.

Minicraft, Unit 1&2, Enterprise City, Meadowfield Avenue, Spennymoor, Durham DL16 6JF
Tel. (01388) 420535
Suppliers of Minicraft tools, although they are readily available at many high street hardware stores and retailers. However, if you contact their head office they may still be able to supply some of the old MB 120 Drills that I so prefer for fine work and which are featured in many of the photographs in this book.

Ashley Iles (Edge Tools) Ltd., East Kirkby, Spilsby, Lincolnshire PE23 4DD
Tel. (01790) 763372   Fax (01790) 763610.
For chisels, gouges and some excellent sharpening materials.

Craft Supplies Ltd., The Mill, Millers Dale, Nr. Buxton, Derbyshire SK17 8SN
Tel. (01298) 871636   Fax (01298) 872263
E-mail: sales@craft-supplies.co.uk
For many tools, plus timbers.

Pintail Decoy Supplies - David and Sheila Clews, 20 Sheppenhall Grove, Aston, Nantwich, Cheshire CW5 8DF
Tel. (01270)780056   Fax (01270) 780056
For carbide, diamond and ruby cutters and lots of other goodies! They can also supply jelutong which they are usually prepared to cut to your own specifications.

Claudius Ash Sons and Co. Ltd., Summit House, Summit Road, Potters Bar, Hertfordshire EN6 3EE
Tel. 0800 090909   Free Phone 0800 090909
Fax (01707) 649901
An excellent source of supply for the very fine diamond burrs that figure prominently in the photographs.

Swann-Morton Ltd., Owlerton Green, Sheffield S6 2BJ
Tel. (0114) 234 4231   Fax (0114) 231 4966
Suppliers of scalpels, knives and blades. I particularly like their SM-00 knife used with the SM01 blade.

General Woodwork Supplies (Stoke Newington) Ltd., 76-80, Stoke Newington High Street, London N16 7PA
Tel. (0171) 254 6052   Fax (0171) 254 722
Suppliers of most timbers, which they will cut to your own requirements. I have for many years used their Brazilian bBoxwood, it is very fine grained, takes stain well and can be brought to an excellent finish. They can usually also supply lemonwood.

John Boddy Timber Ltd., Riverside Sawmills, Boroughbridge, North Yorkshire, YO51 9LJ
Tel. (01423) 322370   Fax (01423) 323810
A good general timber supplier including jelutong.

Timberline, Unit 7, Munday Works, 58 - 66 Morley Road, Tonbridge, Kent TN9 1RP
Tel (01732) 355626   Fax (01732) 358214
Timbers including lemonwood.

Ormiston Wire Ltd., 1 Fleming Way, Worton Road, Isleworth, Middlesex TW7 6EU
Tel.(020) 8569 7287   Fax (020) 8569 8601
E-mail: info@ormiston-wire.co.uk
Suppliers of most types of wire including the tined copper wire that I have made extensive use of on this model.

Lathkill Tackle, Unity Complex, Dale Road North, Darley Dale, Matlock DE4 2HX
Tel: (01629) 735101 Fax (01629) 735648.
E-mail: lathkill.tackle@flytying.demon.co.uk
Suppliers of a good range of the finer threads suitable for miniature rope making.

The Airbrush & Spray Centre Ltd., 39 Littlehampton Road, Worthing, West Sussex BN13 1QJ
Tel. (01903) 266991   Fax (01903) 830045
E-mail: airbrush@lineone.net
All your airbrush needs. They can also supply the Paasche Custom MV#2 mentioned in the text.

H.S. Walsh, 21 St. Cross Street, Hatton Garden,
London EC1N 8UN
Tel. (0171) 2423711
Suppliers of tools for the jewellery trade including
Dumont Tweezers and very fine files.

Primrose Repair Services, Studham Lane, Dagnall,
Berkhamstead, Herts. HP4 1RH
Tel. & Fax (0144) 2842394
For supplies of Seccotine.

In the US

Preac Tool Co., Inc. 1596 Teapond Road, North
Bellmore, New York USA NY 11710
Tel. 001- 516 - 333- 1500   Fax 5116-333-1501
E-Mail: preac@erols.com
For the excellent miniature precision table saw,
thicknesses, etc.

Micro-Mark, 340-2656 Snyder Avenue, Berkeley
Heights NJ 07922
Good supplier of a great variety of tools.

Warner Woods West, P.O. Box 100, Ivins UT 84738
For wood supplies.

Lumber Yard, 6908 Stadium Drive,
Brecksville OH 44141
Has a wide range of woods.

The following are good suppliers of general modelling
materials:

K&S Engineering, 6917 W. 59th Street,
Chicago Il 60638

Small Parts Inc, 13980 NW 58th Court,
Miami Lakes FL 33014

Ace Surgical Supply Co, 1034 Pearl Street,
Brockton MA 02401

Pelican Wire Co, Inc, 6266 Taylor Road,
Naples FL 34109

BIBLIOGRAPHY

Below is a list of a books, periodical and catalogues which I have found useful sources of information during the construction of this and many other models.

Craine, J H, 'Ropes and How to Make Them', *Model Shipwright*, No 2 (1972)

Freeston, Ewart, 'Variations on a Rope making Theme', *Model Shipwright*, No 19 (1975)

Gardiner, Robert (ed), *Nelson against Napoleon: From the Nile to Copenhagen, 1798 - 1801* (London 1997)

Goodwin, Peter, *The Construction and Fitting of the Sailing Man of War 1650 - 1850* (London 1987)

Hahn, Harold M, *Ships of the American Revolution and their Models* (London 1988)

–'Oliver Cromwell/Beavers Prize', *Model Shipwright*, No 19 (1977)

Harland, John, *Seamanship in the Age of Sail* (London 1985)

Howard, Dr Frank, *Sailing Ships of War 1400 - 1860* (London 1979)

Lavery, Brian, *The Ship of the Line: Volume I, The Development of the Battlefleet 1650 - 1850* (London 1983)

The Ship of the Line: Volume II, Design, Construction and Fittings (London 1984)

The 74 -Gun Ship Bellona (London 1985)

Lees, James, *The Masting and Rigging of English Ships of War 1625 - 1860* (London 1979)

Longridge, C Nepean, *The Anatomy of Nelson's Ships* (London 1955)

Marquardt, Karl Heinz, *Eighteenth-Century Rigs and Rigging* (London 1992)

McKay John, *The 100-gun ship Victory* (London 1987)

McKay, John and Coleman, Ron, *The 24-Gun Frigate Pandora* (London 1992)

McNarry, Donald, *Ship Models in Miniature* (Newton Abbot 1975)

– *Shipbuilding in Miniature* (London 1982)

–'Royal Oak (1769)' *Model Shipwright*, No 87 (1994)

Plolak Catalogue 1987, Print of *Nelson's Santa Cruz Squadron at Sea 1797*: by Gardiner, Derek G.M. RSMA.

Purves, Alec A, *Flags For Ship Modellers and Marine Artists* (London 1983)

Underhill, Harold, *Plank-on-Frame Models, Volume I* (Glasgow 1958) and *Volume II* (Glasgow 1960)

White, David, *The Frigate Diana* (London 1987)

Wilson, Timothy, *Flags at Sea* (London 1999)